Acknowledgm

Information was taken from:-

- The Vital Guide to Modern \
  Publishing Ltd, Shrewsbury,
- Seaforth World Naval Review 2010/15, edited by Conrad
  Waters. (Seaforth Publishing, Barnsley, S Yorkshire) ISBN
  978 1 84832 051 2. ISBN 978 1 84832 075 8. ISBN 978 1
  84832 120 5. ISBN 978 1 84832 156 4. ISBN 978 1 84832 182
  3. ISBN 978 1 84832 220 2. ISBN 978 1 84832 309 4.
- The World Encyclopedia of Amphibious Warfare Vessels.
  Bernard Ireland.(Lorenz Books, Anness Publishing Ltd, Blaby
  Road, Wigston Leicestershire LE18 4SE).
- The World Encyclopaedia of Military Helicopters. Francis
  Crosby. (Lorenz Books, Anness Publishing Ltd, Blaby Road,
  Wigston, Leicestershire LE18 4SE).
- The World Encyclopaedia of Fighters and Bombers. Francis
  Crosby. (Southwater books, Anness Publishing Ltd, Blaby
  Road, Wigston, Leicestershire LE18 4SE).
- The World Encyclopaedia of Destroyers, Frigates and
  Submarines. Bernard Ireland and John Parker. (Lorenz Books,
  Anness Publishing Ltd, Blaby Road, Wigston, Leicestershire
  LE18 4SE).
- The World Encyclopaedia of Aircraft Carriers and Naval
  Aircraft. Bernard Ireland and Francis Crosby. (Lorenz Books,
  Anness Publishing Ltd, Blaby Road, Wigston, Leicestershire
  LE18 4SE).
- The Encyclopaedia of Warships. Edited by Robert Jackson.
  (Thunder Bay Press, Advantage Publishers Group, 5880
  Oberon Drive, San Diego, CA 92121-4794). ISBN-13: 978 1
  59223 627 5. ISBN-10: 1 59223 627 8.
- The Illustrated Directory of Modern Soviet Weapons. Edited by
  Ray Bonds. Salamander Books Ltd, 52 Bedford Row, London
  WC1R 4LR, United Kingdom. ISBN 0 86101 252 6.

Introduction

The Chinese navy is known as "The People's Liberation Army Navy" (quite a mouthful) and is one of the youngest navies in the world. It was established in 1950 following China's civil war. Great assistance was given by the Soviet Union in the shape of advisers and technology. The navy, at this point, was a "brown-water" fleet, patrolling the vast inland waterways and the large coastline of China. After the break-up of the Soviet Union and the collapse of the "Red Army", the main reason China had to defend its land borders had gone. Emphasis then switched to China defending itself from the United States. Why it thinks it has to do this, no one really knows. Possibly, it may have something to do with China's friendship with North Korea and the United States friendship with South Korea. In the 1990s, China began to build a fleet capable of challenging the US Navy. This program was accelerated, following several small incidents at sea, where the US Navy, acting as the *global Policeman*, intercepted Chinese ships and the Chinese navy was powerless to respond. The Chinese navy of today is one of massive ongoing construction, rivalling the Soviet Union's naval construction during the Cold War. The Chinese "blue-water" fleet is growing every year with new destroyers, frigates, corvettes, amphibious vessels, patrol boats, submarines and aircraft carriers coming off the production line, it would seem, almost daily. China is also building warships for other nations. Algeria has ordered three destroyers from Chinese shipyards. These vessels are not an extended production run of existing ships but a new design specifically designed for the export market.

This build-up has not gone unnoticed and has put several of China's neighbours under pressure. The biggest local threat to China is India. India has, in turn, begun her own naval build-up to counter China and other regional countries are expanding their fleets. All of this has led to a regional naval arms race, which has been going since the turn of the century. The United States Navy has now turned its attention to China because of the naval build-up and begun its "pivot" to the Pacific. Whereas China never had to defend itself from the US Navy, now it looks as if it might have to.

The Submarine force is beginning to switch from a conventional force to a nuclear one. New "SSBN's" are commissioned and more are in the development stage, to provide China with a sea-borne nuclear deterrent. New classes of "SSN's" are coming off the slipways at an increasing rate. This is alongside new conventional submarines of the "Kilo" class, which are still in production. The number of submarines and different classes which are being built is approaching what the Soviet Union did during the Cold War.

China, at last, has a functioning aircraft carrier to see it through this decade. A new class is under construction with the first due to be launched very soon. It is unknown whether these vessels will be nuclear powered. How many China will build remains to be seen but it will be more than one, as it intendeds to challenge the US Navy's carrier groups.

Destroyers, frigates, corvettes and missile patrol boats are coming off the slipways at an ever-increasing rate. Besides existing programs, new vessels are being designed to replace old tonnage and continue the expansion. The most impressive of these is the new "cruiser" sized destroyers of the "Type 055" class. These ships will be the heaviest armed ships China has ever built and maybe be second only to the "Kirov" battlecruisers, for weaponry. The ships themselves will match the new "Leader" class, which Russia is intending to build. These vessels are the clearest indication of China's intentions about deploying Carrier Battle Groups, with very powerful and multi-capable escorts. It would not be a surprise if these "cruisers", will soon have a sub-class, which are nuclear powered. US experience has shown that nuclear carriers need nuclear escorts, which can match their endurance. The US has not built nuclear escorts since the end of the Cold War owing to the cost. Cost, at the moment, does not seem to bother the Chinese.

The amphibious assault fleet is expanding with new "Dock Landing Ships" that are entering service and even a new class of "flat-top" assault ships. These will match the US Navy's "flat-top" assault ships in size and capability. How many of these will be built is still not clear. Large numbers of new "Tank Landing Ships" are also being built to replace old tonnage and to expand the fleet. All of these amphibious programs and construction must be making Taiwan very nervous.

The replenishment fleet is also being expanded with new large supply ships being launched, as well as submarine tenders, cargo ships etc. All of these are to augment the "blue-water" capability, which China is building.

The "naval air arm" is also being expanded in preparation for the new carriers and also the large number of other surface warships that are capable of handling helicopters.

This naval expansion, to many people, is astonishing considering China is not at war. With the Chinese defence budget rising by 167% in 2015/2016, many are wondering what the reason, or reasons, behind this are. One is that China genuinely feels threatened by the US Navy and other regional powers, two, building weapons and having a large military is the easiest way to keep an economy healthy and to provide jobs to its billion and a half citizens, three, they are preparing to invade Taiwan and settle some old scores with some old enemies. China is claiming almost all of the South China Sea as its own and a large chunk of the Western Pacific. It is creating "island bastions" in these areas and is constantly warning off foreign warships from waters that have always been open to transit. These "bastions" are equipped with an airstrip and naval facilities, plus a garrison. This is the same thing the Japanese Empire did in World War 2. Any attacking nation would have to deal with the "island chain" before getting to the Chinese mainland.

This is beginning to harden other countries attitudes towards China and will do nothing to defuse the situation. Recently, Japan has changed its pacifist constitution to allow it to build offensive forces. Only one percent of its GDP is for defence spending, therefore this can easily be raised to deal with the Chinese threat. New coastal weapon emplacements are being constructed along Japan's Western coast. These are areas where the Chinese Navy has to transit to reach the open Pacific making for an even more tense situation.

Surely, the Chinese leadership can see what effect the military build-up is having on the region and it seems that they just do not care. This the same thing the Soviet Union did during the Cold War.
Regardless of the reason, it is very impressive to watch, if a little scary.

[2]"Naval Ensign"

Source https://commons.wikimedia.org/wiki/File:Naval_Ensign_of_the_People%27s_Republic_of_China.svg

Pennant Numbers

Ship	Pennant Number	Ship	Pennant Number
Nuclear Ballistic Missile Submarines		**Diesel-Electric Submarines cont'd**	
Changzheng 6	406	?	352
Changzheng 8	408	?	353
Changzheng 9	409	?	354
?	?	?	356
?	?	?	357
		?	358
Nuclear Attack Submarines		?	359
		?	360
Changzheng 3	403	?	361
Changzheng 4	404	?	362
Changzheng 5	405	?	363
Changzheng 7	407	Yuan Zhend 64 Hao	364
Changzheng 10	410	Yuan Zhend 65 Hao	365
?	?	Yuan Zheng 66 Hao	366
?	?	Yuan Zheng 67 Hao	367
?	?	Yuan Zheng 68 Hao	368
?*	?	Yuan Zheng 69 Hao	369
		Yuan Zheng 70 Hao	370
Diesel-Electric Submarine		Yuan Zheng 71 Hao	371
		Yuan Zheng 72 Hao	372
?	305	Yuan Zheng 73 Hao	373
?	306	Yuan Zheng 74 Hao	374
?	307	Yuan Zheng 75 Hao	375
?	308		
?	309	**Experimental Submarine**	
?	310	Qing?	201
?	320		
?	321	**Aircraft Carriers**	
?	322	Liaoning	16
?	323	?*	17
?	324	?*	18
?	325		
?	314	**Amphibious Assault Ships**	
?	315		
?	316	Tai Shan*	978
?	326	Tanggula Shan*	979
?	327	Yimen Shan	988
?	328	Changbai Shan	989
?	329		

*still under construction

Ship	Pennant Number	Ship	Pennant Number
Amphibious Assault Ships cont'd		**Tank Landing Ships cont'd**	
Kunlun Shan	998	Daiyun Shan	994
Jinggang Shan	999	Wangang Shan	995
		Laotie Shan	996
Tank Landing Ships		Luhua Shan	997
Yandang Shan	908		3111
Jiuhua Shan	909		3113
Huanggang Shan	910		3115
Tianzhu Shan	911		3116
Daqing Shan	912		3117
Baxian Shan	913		3128
Yuntai Shan	927		3129
Wufeng Shan	928		3229
Zijin Shan	929		3232
Lingyan Shan	930		3233
Dongting Shan	931		3234
Helan Shan	932		3235
Liupan Shan	933		3244
Danxia Shan	934		7593
Xuefeng Shan	935		7594
Haiyang Shan	936		7595
Qingcheng Shan	937		
Putuo Shan	939	**Landing Craft**	
Tiantai Shan	940	Yunnan class	
Sheng Shan	941	Zubr class	
Lu Shan	942	LCAC 716 class	
?	943	LCAC 722 class	
Yu Shan	944	LCAC 724 class	
Hua Shan	945	LCAC 726 class	
Song Shan	946		
?	947	**Destroyers**	
Xue Shan	948	?*	100?
Heng Shan	949	?*	101?
Tai Shan	950	Kaifeng	109
?*	981	Dalian	110
?*	982	Harbin	112
?*	983	Qingdao	113
Wudang Shan	990	Shenyang	115
Emei Shan	991	Shijiazhuang	116
Huading Shan	992	Xining	117
Luoxiao Shan	993	Taiyuan*	118

*still under construction

Ship	Pennant Number	Ship	Pennant Number
Destroyers cont'd		**Frigates cont'd**	
?*	119	Dandong	543
?*	120	Linfen	545
Zunyi	134	Yan Cheng	546
Hangzhou	136	Lin Yi	547
Fuzhou	137	Yi Yang	548
Taizhou	138	Chang Zhou	549
Ningbo	139	Wei Fang	550
Changchun	150	Shaoguan	553
Zhengzhou	151	Zhaotong	555
Jinan	152	Beihai	558
Xi'an*	153	Foshan	559
Xiamen*	154	Dongguan	560
Guiyang*	155	Shantou	561
?*	156	Jiangmen	562
?*	157	Zhoaqing	563
Nanchang	163	Yichang	564
Guilin	164	Huludao	565
Zhanjiang	165	Huaihua	566
Zhuhai	166	Xiangyang	567
Shenzhen	167	Heng Yang	568
Guangzhou	168	Yu Lin	569
Wuhan	169	Huang Shan	570
Lanzhou	170	Yun Cheng	571
Haikou	171	Heng Shui	572
		Liu Zhou	573
Frigates		San Ya	574
Jiaxing	521	Yue Yang	575
Lianyungang	522	Da Qing	576
Putian	523	Huang Gang	577
Sanming	524	Yang Zhou	578
Ma'anshan	525	Han Dan	579
Wenshou	526		
Luoyang	527	**Corvettes**	
Mianyang	528	Xinyang	501
Zhou Shan	529	Huangshi	502
Xu Zhou	530	Suzhou	503
Taizhou	533	Saqian	504
Jinhoa	534	?*	505
Cangzhou	537	?*	512
Yan Tai	538	Datong	580
Tongling	542	Yingkou	581

*still under construction

Ship	Pennant Number	Ship	Pennant Number
Corvettes cont'd		**Minesweepers cont'd**	
Bengbu	582	Kunshan	818
Shangrao	583	Liuyang	839
Meizhou	584	Luxi	840
Baise	585	Xiaoyi	841
Ji'an	586	Taishan	842
Jieyang	587	Changshu	843
Quanzhou	588	Heshan	844
Qingyuan	589	Qingzhou	845
Weihai	590	Yucheng	846
Fu Shun	591		
Luzhou	592	**Replenishment Ships**	
Sanmenxia	593	Hongzehu	881
Zhouzhou	594	Poyanghu	882
Chaozhou	595	Dongtinghu	883
Huizhou	596	Jingpohu	884
Qinzhou	597	Qinghaihu	885
?*	598	Qingdaohu	886
?*	599	Weishanhu	887
		Fuxianhu	888
Patrol Boats		Taihu	889
Yangjiang	770	Chaohu	890
Shunde	771	Dongpinghu	960
Nanhai	772	junshanhu	961
Panyu	773	Luguhu	962
Lianjiang	774	?	963
Xinhui	775	?	965
Houbei class		Gaoyaohu	966
Shanghai III class			
Hainan class		**Cargo Ships**	
Haiqing class		Yuan Wang	21
Houxin class		Yuan Wang	22
		Yantai class	
Minesweepers		Bei-Yun	443
?	800	Bei-Yun	528
Xiangshan	801	Dong-Yun	577
?	802	Dong-Yun	7656
?	803	Dong-Yun	771
Huoqin	804	Nan-Yun	835
Zhangjiangang	805	Nan-Yun	836
?	806	Galati class	
Jingjiang	810	Danlin class	

*still under construction

Ship	Pennant Number	Ship	Pennant Number
Cargo Ships cont'd		**Barracks Ship**	
Dandao class		Xu Xiake	88
Troop & Cargo Ships		**Tracking Ships**	
Nan-Yun	830	Yuan Wang	3
Nan-Yun	831	Yuan Wang	5
Nan-Yun	832	Yuan Wang	6
Nan-Yun	833		
Nan-Yun	834		
Nan-Yun	835	**Intelligence Ships**	
		North Star	851
Coastal Tankers		Beijixing	851
Leizhou class		Haiwangxing	852
Shengli class		Tianwangxing	853
Fulin class		?	856
Fuzhou class		Bei-Diao	900
Jinyou class			
Bei-You	565	**Research Ships**	
Dong-You	631	Haiyang	1
Dong-You	641	Haiyang	2
Dong-Shui	646	Haiyang	3
Dong-Shui	647	Haiyang	4
Nan-You	957	Haiyang	11
Nan-You	958	Haiyang	12
Nan-You	959	Kexue	1
Nan-You	973	Shiian	3
		Xiangyanghong	01
Hospital Ships		Xiangyanghong	02
Zhuanghe	865	Xiangyanghong	03
Dai san dao hao	866	Xiangyanghong	07
Beiyi class		xiangyanghong	08
		Xiangyanghong 4	223
Multi-role Ship		Xiangyanghong 6	485
Shichang	82	Xiangyanghong 9	350
		Bei-Ce	943
Training Ship		Dong-Ce	227
Zhenghe	81	Dong-Ce	226
		Nan-Ce	427
Icebreakers		Nan-Ce	420
Haibing	722	Hai-Sheng	582
Haidao	723	Zhu Kezhen	872
Haibing	519	Qian Sanqiang	873

*still under construction

Ship	Pennant Number	Ship	Pennant Number
Environmental Research Ships		**Torpedo Retrieval Ships**	
Bei-Jian	10	Bei-Yun	455
Dong-Jian	01	Bei-Yun	484
Dong-Jian	02	Bei-Yun	485
Nan-Jian	01	Bei-Yun	529
Nan-Jian	02	Dong-Yun	758
Nan-Jian	03	Dong-Yun	803
		Nan-Yun	841
Submarine Repair Ship			
Dong-Xiu	911	**Diving Tenders**	
		Kancha	1
Submarine Rescue Ships		Kancha	2
Bei-Jiu	137	**Degaussing Ships**	
Dong-Jiu	304	Nan-Qin	202
Nan-Jiu	502	Nan-Qin	203
Hai-Jiu	512	Nan-Qin	205
		Bei-Qin	731
Submarine Support Ships		Bei-Qin	735
		Bei-Qin	736
Changxingdao	121	Dong-Qin	860
Chongxingdao	302	Dong-Qin	863
Yongxingdao	506	Dong-Qin	864
Yongxingdao	863	Dong-Qin	870
Oceanic Island	864		
Liugong Island	865	**Rescue Ships**	
Long Island	867	Bei-Jiu	122
		Bei-Jiu	138
Weapon Testing Ships		Bei-Jiu	143
Bi Sheng	891	Dong-Jiu	332
Hua Luogeng	892	Dong-Jiu	335
Zhan Tianyou	893	Hai-Jiu	403
Li Siguang	894	Nan-Jiu	503
		Nan-Jiu	510
Sonar Testing Ship			
Beidiao	993		
Torpedo Trials Ships			
Kancha	3		
Kancha	4		

*still under construction

Ship	Pennant Number	Ship	Pennant Number
Cable Layers		Bei-Tuo	712
	B230	Bei-Tuo	716
	B233	Bei-Tuo	717
	B234	Dong-Tuo	518
	B764	Dong-Tuo	604
	B765	Dong-Tuo	613
	B873	Dong-Tuo	618
	B874	Dong-Tuo	646
		Dong-Tuo	707
Buoy Tenders		Dong-Tuo	802
Dongbiao	263	Dong-Tuo	809
Nanbiao	463	Dong-Tuo	811
Beibiao	982	Dong-Tuo	813
Beibiao	983	Dong-Tuo	822
		Dong-Tuo	824
Ocean-Going Tugs		Dong-Tuo	827
Nan-Tuo	147	Dong-Tuo	830
Nan-Tuo	149	Dong-Tuo	836
Bei-Tuo	153	Dong-Tuo	837
Nan-Tuo	154	Dong-Tuo	842
Nan-Tuo	155	Dong-Tuo	843
Nan-Tuo	156	Dong-Tuo	852
Nan-Tuo	156	Dong-Tuo	853
Bei-Tuo	159	Dong-Tuo	854
Nan-Tuo	161	Dong-Tuo	862
Bei-Tuo	162	Dong-Tuo	863
Bei-Tuo	163	Dong-Tuo	867
Bei-Tuo	164	Dong-Tuo	875
Nan-Tuo	164	Dong-Tuo	877
Nan-Tuo	166	Dong-Tuo	890
Nan-Tuo	167		
Bei-Tuo	168		
Nan-Tuo	174		
Nan-Tuo	175		
Nan-Tuo	185		
Bei-Tuo	622		
Bei-Tuo	635		
Bei-Tuo	680		
Bei-Tuo	683		
Bei-Tuo	684		
Bei-Tuo	710		
Bei-Tuo	711		

*still under construction

Nuclear Powered Ballistic Missile Submarines

"Jin" class "Type 094"

[3]"Type 094" boat

defenceforumindia.com

Name	Pennant	Completed	Builder
Changzheng 8	408	2010?	Bohai Shipyard
Changzheng 9	409	2013?	Bohai Shipyard
?	?	2013?	Bohai Shipyard
?	?	2015?	Bohai Shipyard

Displacement. 8,000 tonnes   **Dimensions.** 132.89m x 12.5m x 9.14m
Speed. 25 knots   **Complement.** 120
Armament. 6 x 533mm Torpedo tubes; 12 or 16 x JL-2 Ballistic Missiles

Notes

This class of "SSBN" are the first, fully operational, Chinese "Ballistic Missile Submarines". Owing to China's secrecy, the first "Type 094", was not spotted until 2006 by a spy satellite. Two more were spotted in 2007 but it is not clear whether this included the first one. Owing to this, it is not known whether there are actually four or five active boats.

Earlier boats carry 12 "Ballistic Missile's", while latter boats have been lengthened to carry 16. These missiles are the "JL-2", which have a range of between 8,000kms and 12,000kms. This puts the USA, India and even Western Europe within range, from Chinese home waters.

The first "strategic" patrols were due to have taken place in 2015, with deployments to the Pacific and Indian Oceans.

---

[3]
  Source http://defenceforumindia.com/forum/threads/china-military-photos-videos.3157/page-133

"Xia" class "Type 092"

[4]"Xia" class

defenceforumindia.com

Name	Pennant	Completed	Builder
Changzheng 6	406	1987	Bohai Shipyard

Displacement. 6,500 tonnes   **Dimensions.** 120m x 10m x 8m
Speed. 22 knots   **Complement.** 100
Armament. 6 x 533mm Torpedo tubes; 12 x JL-1A Ballistic Missiles

Notes
This "SSBN", has been based on the "Type 091" class of nuclear attack submarine. She was laid down in 1978 and launched in 1981. She spent the next six years fitting out, testing equipment and conducting sea-trials before entering service in 1987. Since then, she has been refitted several times with more advanced sonars, machinery and weaponry. She is China's first "Ballistic Missile Submarine" and is the forerunner, for the "Type 094" class.
She has been based at Jianggezhuang, near Qingdao, since entering service and has never conducted a "strategic" or "deterrent" patrol, outside Chinese regional seas. According to latest reports, she is no longer active in the "strategic" role. China is very secretive about her submarine programs and rarely puts them on the world stage. "Changzheng" did, however, make an appearance at the PLA's sixtieth anniversary event in 2009.

"Tang" class "Type 096"

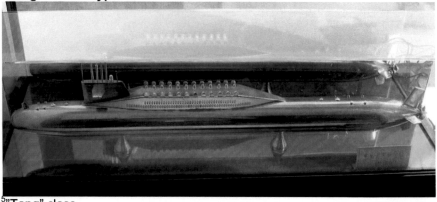

[5]"Tang" class

Midgetman433

The "Tang" class is believed to be under development as the next generation of Nuclear Ballistic Missile Submarines of the Chinese Navy. Western sources believe it will have, approximately, the same displacement and dimensions of Western and Russian "SSBN's". Instead of 12 or 16 Ballistic missiles of previous boats, they will carry 24 "JL-3" missiles. There are reports that at least one boat may already have been launched.

"Type 098"

No Photo available

This is the very latest Chinese "SSBN", which is reported to be under development. It is reported to be about the same size as a US Navy "Ohio" class and be able to carry 24 Ballistic missiles. If this is true, then the Chinese Navy will soon begin to have as many submarines in production and development as the Soviet Union did at the height of the Cold War.

5
  Source https://en.wikipedia.org/wiki/File:Tang_type-96.jpg

Nuclear Attack Submarines

"Shang" class "Type 093"

[6]"Shang" class

defenceforumindia.com

Name	Pennant	Completed	Builder
Changzheng 7	407	2006	Bohai Shipyard
Changzheng 10	410	2009	Bohai Shipyard
?	?	2015?	Bohai Shipyard
?	?	2015?	Bohai Shipyard
?	?	2015?	Bohai Shipyard
?	?	Expected 2017	Bohai Shipyard

Displacement. 7,000 tonnes   **Dimensions.** 110m x 11m x 7.5m
Speed. 30 knots   **Complement.** 100
Armament. 6 x 533mm or 650mm Torpedo tubes; YJ-18 VLS anti-ship missiles

Notes
This class of "SSN" is the follow-on design of the "Type 092" class. They are the first class of Chinese "nuclear attack submarines", which can compete with Western and Russian "SSN's".

---

[6]
Source http://defenceforumindia.com/forum/threads/china-military-photos-videos.3157/page-134

Development of these boats began in 1994, after tensions with Taiwan increased and US involvement in the "Yinhe" incident, in 1993. As the Cold War had just ended, the US fleet was still huge and China had nothing to challenge it. This was the beginning of Chinese naval expansion.

The weapon suite is open to question. Some reports suggest that conventional sized torpedo tubes of 533mm have been fitted but others say that the bigger 650mm sized tubes have been fitted. The Russian's have 650mm tubes for their "carrier killer" torpedoes but these tubes are fitted alongside regular sized tubes. It is more likely that a combination of tubes have been installed. A "Vertical Launch System" has also been fitted, which is in the US "Los Angeles" class of "SSN", for the "YJ-18" anti-ship missile. How many missiles are carried is not known.

Two boats have been active since the last decade, with three more ready for delivery by 2015. A sixth is reported to be under construction.

The "Shang's" will replace the "Type 091" on a one-for-one basis and probably exceed them. It is likely however, that production will stop at six boats owing to the development of the "Type 095" class.

[7]"Shang" class

"Han" class "Type 091"

[8]"Han" class

Name	Pennant	Completed	Builder
Changzheng 3	403	1984	Bohai Shipyard
Changzheng 4	404	1988	Bohai Shipyard
Changzheng 5	405	1990	Bohai Shipyard

Displacement. 5,500 tonnes   **Dimensions.** 98m x 10m x 7.4m
Speed. 25 knots   **Complement.** 75
Armament. 6 x 533mm Torpedo tubes

Notes
This class of "SSN" is the first nuclear powered attack submarines deployed by the Chinese Navy. They were designed and built in China and were also the first nuclear powered submarines to be built in Asia. Five boats were commissioned in total. The first was completed in 1974 and decommissioned in 2000. She is now a museum. The second was commissioned in 1980 and decommissioned 2004. The last three are still active but will soon be replaced by the "Shang" class.

Their design is quite basic, compared to Western and Russian boats. More importantly, their reactors are not to Western standards and are very noisy with very little radiation shielding which does present a great hazard to the crew.

Source http://defenceforumindia.com/forum/threads/china-military-photos-videos.3157/page-145

These boats are well armed, with six torpedo tubes and at least twenty torpedoes. Anti-ship missiles can be fired but only if they are on or near the surface, making them very vulnerable to detection.

Until the mid 1990s, the "Han" class operated in mainly Chinese regional waters, however, since then the "Han's" have gone further afield and flexed their muscle against American and Japanese naval forces.

[9]"Han" class

defenceforumindia.com

"Type 095" class

No Photo available.

A new class of "Nuclear Attack Submarine" began development at the beginning of the last decade. It is third generation design, after the "Type 093". They have a more advanced nuclear reactor and are very much quieter than previous boats. New active passive and flank sonar's have been fitted.
There is very little detail about displacement and dimensions, along with the type of weapon suite but it is very likely it will be almost the same as the previous "Shang" class. Some sources compare them to the Russian "Akula" class "SSN's".
Some reports suggest that two boats, out of a planned 12, have been launched by 2015 and may even have begun sea-trials. These boats, along with the "Shang" class, are more than capable of acting as carrier escorts, in the same way as the US Navy deploys its nuclear submarines.

Diesel-Electric Submarines

"Song" class "Type 039"

[10]"Song" class

SteKruebe

Name	Pennant	Completed	Builder
?	320	1999	Wuhan Shipyard
?	321	2001	Wuhan Shipyard
?	322	2001	Wuhan Shipyard
?	323	2003	Wuhan Shipyard
?	324	2003	Wuhan Shipyard
?	325	2004	Wuhan Shipyard
?	314	2004	Wuhan Shipyard
?	315	2004	Wuhan Shipyard
?	316	2005	Wuhan Shipyard
?	326	2005	Wuhan Shipyard
?	327	2006	Wuhan Shipyard
?	328	2005	Wuhan Shipyard
?	329	2006	Wuhan Shipyard

Displacement. 2,250 tonnes
Speed. 22 knots
Armament. 6 x 533mm Torpedo tubes

Dimensions. 74.9m x 8.4m x 5.3m
Complement. 60

---

[10] Source https://commons.wikimedia.org/wiki/File:Song-class_Submarine_5.jpg

Notes

This large class of diesel-electric submarine is the first Chinese submarine completely designed and built in China. Even their weaponry is Chinese built. They are designed to attack shipping and are also capable of engaging other submarines. Their machinery is very quiet, compared to other Chinese built submarines before and they also have sound absorbing tiles fixed to the hull. The first boat, "320", was completed almost three years before the second, to allow systems to be tested and to iron out any problems. In fact, so many problems were found that all of the subsequent boats were built to a slightly different specification and are sometimes referred to as a separate class.

The weapon suite is of Chinese origin, with eighteen, "Yu-4" torpedoes being carried. The "YJ-8" anti-ship missile can be carried and fired from the torpedo tubes.

It has been reported that Thailand had shown some interest in acquiring an export version of the "Song" class but this did not happen.

[11]"Song" class

defenceforumindia.com

Source http://defenceforumindia.com/forum/threads/china-military-photos-videos.3157/page-26

"Kilo" class

[12]"Kilo" class

Name	Pennant	Completed	Builder
Yuan Zhend 64 Hao	364	1994	Nizhniy Novgorod
Yuan Zhend 65 Hao	365	1995	Nizhniy Novgorod
Yuan Zheng 66 Hao	366	1997	Saint Petersburg
Yuan Zheng 67 Hao	367	1998	Saint Petersburg
Yuan Zheng 68 Hao	368	2004	Saint Petersburg
Yuan Zheng 69 Hao	369	2005	Saint Petersburg
Yuan Zheng 70 Hao	370	2005	Saint Petersburg
Yuan Zheng 71 Hao	371	2005	Saint Petersburg
Yuan Zheng 72 Hao	372	2006	Saint Petersburg
Yuan Zheng 73 Hao	373	2005	Nizhniy Novgorod
Yuan Zheng 74 Hao	374	2005	Severodvinsk
Yuan Zheng 75 Hao	375	2005	Severodvinsk

---

[12]
Source http://defenceforumindia.com/forum/threads/china-military-photos-videos.3157/page-52

Displacement. 2,350 tonnes   **Dimensions.** 74m x 9.9m x 6.5m
Speed. 25 knots   **Complement.** 52
Armament. 6 x 533mm Torpedo tubes, plus 18 reloads

Notes
This very large class of conventionally powered submarines have been a great success. Not only have they been constructed in large numbers for the Soviet/Russian Navy but also they have achieved excellent export sales. Construction began in 1979 at a rate of one boat per year. This soon increased to two per year as the shipyards became familiar with the design. The "Kilo,s" have a teardrop hull, which is a break from previous Soviet designs. They were initially constructed in the Far East, on the Pacific coast, presumably to operate in the Sea of Okhotsk, protecting Soviet "SSBN's", which operated there. As the export market to Soviet satellite states began to increase, they were constructed in the West. Twenty "Kilo"s are currently active within the Russian fleet. Some of these are in reserve but still have skeleton crews aboard. So far, only two Russian boats are known to have been decommissioned and scrapped. Those are "B405" and "B470". India has been the biggest customer for the original "Kilo" design, with at least nine boats, Iran received three, while China and Algeria each received two. Poland and Romania each had one boat. Most of these have been modernized and are still active. India lost one boat due to an explosion whilst at Mumbai dockyard. Eighteen sailors were killed and the submarine destroyed.
A new variant began to be laid down in 1996 for export to China. Ten of these were ordered, with the first entering service in 1997 and the last in 2005. Algeria also ordered two boats and these entered service in 2009. The Russian Navy has ordered six of these boats to begin replacing the original "Kilo"s, which are still in service but are reaching the end of their service lives. Two of these are already in commission. Vietnam has ordered six boats and these began to enter service in 2014, with it anticipated to have them all in service by the end of 2016.

[13]Improved "Kilo" class   Mike1979Russia

[13] Source https://commons.wikimedia.org/wiki/File:Improved_Kilo_class_SS.svg

"Yuan" class "Type 039A"

[14]"Yuan" class

defenceforumindia.com

Name	Pennant	Completed	Builder
?	327	2008	Wuhan Shipyard
?	328	2009	Wuhan Shipyard
?	329	2010	Wuhan Shipyard
?	330	2011	Wuhan Shipyard
?	331	2012	Wuhan Shipyard
?	332	2012	Wuhan Shipyard
?	333	2013	Wuhan Shipyard
?	334	2013	Wuhan Shipyard
?	335?	2014?	Wuhan Shipyard
?	336?	2014?	Wuhan Shipyard
?	337?	2014?	Wuhan Shipyard
?	338?	2015?	Wuhan Shipyard
?	339?	2015?	Wuhan Shipyard
?	340?	2015?	Wuhan Shipyard
?	341?	2015?	Wuhan Shipyard

Displacement. 3,600 tonnes **Dimensions.** 77.6m x 8.4m x 6.7m
Speed. 20 knots **Complement.** 38
Armament. 6 x 533mm Torpedo tubes

Notes
This large class of diesel-electric submarines are the follow-on design of the "Song" class. In some circles, they are referred to as the "Type 39A" but are often known as the "Type 041".

---

[14] Source http://defenceforumindia.com/forum/threads/china-military-photos-videos.3157/page-52

According to which source or article you read, there are as many as fifteen in service with the Chinese navy and at least another five are planned or being constructed.

They are the first Chinese submarines to be propelled by an "Air Independent Propulsion" system. This allows the boat to remain submerged for up to three weeks at a time. This has also enabled these boats to be one of the quietest diesel-electric submarines in service, anywhere in the world. The hull is a "teardrop" shape and covered with noise absorbing, rubber tiles. The machinery is also much quieter than the "Song" class.

China has offered a smaller, export version of this submarine on the open market. Pakistan has agreed to purchase eight of these boats, with construction to be split between Chinese and Pakistani shipyards.

[15]"Yuan" class

Darkranch23

---

[15] Source https://commons.wikimedia.org/wiki/File:Chinese_Type_093_submarine.jpg

"Ming" class "Type 033"

[16]"Ming" class

Name	Pennant	Completed	Builder
?	352	1988	Wuchang Shipyard
?	353	1989	Wuchang Shipyard
?	354	1990	Wuchang Shipyard
?	356	1991	Wuchang Shipyard
?	357	1992	Wuchang Shipyard
?	358	1993	Wuchang Shipyard
?	359	1994	Wuchang Shipyard
?	360	1995	Wuchang Shipyard
?	361	1995	Wuchang Shipyard
?	362	1996	Wuchang Shipyard
?	363	1996	Wuchang Shipyard
?	305	1998	Wuchang Shipyard
?	306	1998	Wuchang Shipyard
?	307	1999	Wuchang Shipyard
?	308	1999	Wuchang Shipyard
?	309	2000	Wuchang Shipyard
?	310	2001	Wuchang Shipyard

Displacement. 2,110 tonnes   **Dimensions.** 76m x 7.6m x 5.1m
Speed. 18 knots   **Complement.** 57
Armament. 8 x 533mm Torpedo tubes

Notes
The Soviet Union completed construction of the "Romeo" class between 1957 and 1961. The Soviets planned to build 56 in total but this was curtailed at 20 boats because of the switch to nuclear powered submarines.
The "Ming" class is the Chinese version of the Soviet built, "Romeo" class. The Chinese navy originally operated 84 boats. These boats were constructed in Chinese shipyards, under "Sino-Soviet treaty of friendship" and are known as "Type 033". The Soviet Union simply gave China the blueprints and the Chinese built them.
In the 1970s, China began to develop an improved version, which continued into the 1980s. Several boats were constructed in the 1970s and 80s but the boats which are in service today are to an improved design known as "Type 035G".
Latest reports estimated that at least 17 are still in service but it is more than likely this number will have reduced by the time this book is published.

[17]"Ming" class   defenceforumindia.com

Experimental Submarine

"Qing" class "Type 032"

[18]"Qing"

defenceforumindia.com

Name	Pennant	Completed	Builder
Qing?	201	2012	Wuhan Shipyard

Displacement. 3,797 tonnes   **Dimensions.** 92.6m x 10m x 6.85m
Speed. 14 knots   **Complement.** 88
Armament. 1 x 533mm & 1 x 650mm Torpedo tubes
   3 x Ballistic Missiles tubes & 4 x VLS cruise missile tubes

Notes
This diesel-electric submarine is used to test the Chinese Navy's conventional submarine weapons and nuclear weapon systems. It is thought to be the largest conventional submarine in the world, with a submerged displacement of 6,628 tonnes.
The crew of 88 is augmented by 100 scientists when the boat is testing equipment. The 533mm torpedo tube is located on the port side, while the 650mm torpedo tube is on the starboard side. The cruise missile tubes are located forward of the fin, while the three Ballistic missile tubes are in the fin. They are long enough to go from the keel to the top of the fin, (like the "Golf" class submarines). There is also a compartment for special forces and unmanned "ROV's".

---

[18] Source http://defenceforumindia.com/forum/threads/china-military-photos-videos.3157/page-52

Aircraft Carriers

"Liaoning" class

[19]"Varyag"   US Navy

Name	Pennant	Completed	Builder
Liaoning	16	2012	Nikolayev South. Dalian Shipyard

Displacement. 53,050 tonnes **Dimensions.** 304.5m x 75m x 8.97m
Speed. 32 knots **Complement.** 2,626
Armament. 3 x Type 1030 CIWS; 3 x 18 cell HHQ-10 SAM
            2 x ASW rocket launchers
Aircraft. 36

Notes
This aircraft carrier has had one of the most chequered beginnings imaginable. She is a relic of the Cold War. Her keel was laid in 1985 at Shipyard 444 in the Ukraine. She is the second vessel of the Russian "Kuznetsov" class. She was to have been "Riga" but this was changed in 1990 to "Varyag". Following the collapse of the Soviet Union and the ending of the Cold War, construction ceased in 1992. By this time, she had been launched and was at the fitting-out stage. Ownership was passed to the Ukraine government because funding for

---

[19] Source https://commons.wikimedia.org/wiki/File:USNWC_Varyag02.jpg?uselang=en-gb

the new Russian Navy was almost non-existent. The Ukraine government was also in the same position and immediately began searching for a buyer. China showed an interest but declined to purchase the vessel, due to the, then current, political situation. In 1996, a private Chinese citizen named Xu Zengping, showed interest in buying the ship and refitting her as a floating casino. In 1998, the deal was closed and transfer begun. This has since emerged to be a cover story to allay Ukrainian and United States fears about China acquiring an aircraft carrier. Strange when you consider that China had already purchased two of the old "Kiev" class aircraft carriers.

After an eventful journey, which took five months and where she broke loose from her tow, she arrived at Dalian Shipyard to begin her fitting-out. All of her original weapons were removed and replaced with point-defence, weapon systems. Her air-group will most likely consist of 24 fast jets and about a dozen helicopters. The original bow, "ski-jump", has been kept, for launching aircraft, with the arrester wires for landing. It has taken a full, ten years to complete her, with handing over to the navy being conducted in 2012.

In 2015, Xu Zengping had confirmed that he has had no re-imbursement from the Chinese government and that the entire deal had cost him personally $120 million.

Due to the ship's age, it is very likely that "Liaoning", will be used as a training carrier to get pilots ready for the new class of aircraft carriers, which the Chinese have begun to construct.

[20]"Liaoning"

[20] Source http://defenceforumindia.com/forum/threads/china-military-photos-videos.3157/page-78

Future Aircraft Carriers

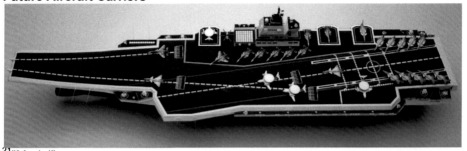

[21]"Model"

defenceforumindia.com

Name	Pennant	Completed	Builder
?	17	Expected 2019	Dalian Shipyard
?	18	Expected 2020	Jiangnan Shipyard

China has begun construction of its first indigenous, designed and built, aircraft carrier. There are reported to be at least two under construction, with the first being laid down in 2015 and the second in 2016. Some sources have stated that there will be a minimum of three carriers built and based at Qingdao naval base. Their displacement is likely to be between 65 to 70,000 tonnes. Dimensions will be, almost, the same size as the "Liaoning". Aircraft numbers are likely to be around fifty machines. There will a "ski-jump", built on to the bow and no catapults positioned there. There will however, be waist catapults to aid in the launching of larger "Airborne Early Warning", aircraft. Recovery of all aircraft will still be done by arrester wire. It has yet to be confirmed whether these ships are to be nuclear powered or conventional. Owing to China's recent military expenditure, it does seem like that they will be nuclear powered. It has come as no surprise that these vessels are being built, when you consider the gradual steps, which have taken place. In 1985, China bought the old British built, "HMAS Melbourne", from Australia. This carrier was studied and dismantled, as a research project. A working replica of her catapults and arrester wires were built for pilots to train on. In the early 1990s, two Soviet "Kiev" class carrier/cruiser hybrids were purchased. These were studied and then turned into floating museums. In the late 1990s, the "Varyag" arrived and this time the Chinese completed her construction, renaming her "Liaoning" and she became China's first working aircraft carrier. In 1995/1996, China began negotiating with Spain, to acquire a Spanish design for a conventional take-off and landing aircraft carrier. Even though the deal did not officially succeed, some reports suggest that there was some kind of design transfer.

---

[21] Source http://defenceforumindia.com/forum/threads/china-military-photos-videos.3157/page-49

Amphibious Assault Ships

"Yuzhoa" class "Type 071"

[22]"Changbai Shan"   kees torn

Name	Pennant	Completed	Builder
Kunlun Shan	998	2007	Hudong
Jinggang Shan	999	2011	Hudong
Changbai Shan	989	2012	Hudong
Yimen Shan	988	2015	Hudong
Tai Shan	978	2017?	Hudong
Tanggula Shan	979	2019?	Hudong

Displacement. 25,000 tonnes   **Dimensions.** 210m x 28m x 7m
Speed. 25 knots   **Complement.** 120
Armament. 1 x 76mm gun; 4 x 30mm AK-630 CIWS
Aircraft. 4 x helicopters
Landing Craft. 4 LCAC

Notes
These six vessels are amphibious "Dock Landing Ships". They are the Chinese
Navy's equivalent of the US Navy's "San Antonio" class. These vessels have
about the same displacement and dimensions. They have the ability to carry
and put ashore 800 troops and their equipment. The vehicle deck is able to
accommodate over twenty armoured vehicles of various sizes. All of the heavy
equipment can be put ashore using the four "Air-cushioned Landing Craft". They

---

[22] Source https://commons.wikimedia.org/wiki/File:PLANS_Changbaishan_(LSD-989)_20150130(2).jpg

are able to carry a main battle tank or several lighter vehicles. The troops and lighter equipment can be transported using the four medium to heavy lift helicopters, which are embarked.

These ships give the Chinese navy a truly "out-of-area" capability, to land and support troops in a large-scale amphibious operation. The first four vessels are in service with the fifth and sixth under construction.

[23]"Jinggang Shan"

defenceforumindia.com

23 Source http://defenceforumindia.com/forum/threads/china-military-photos-videos.3157/page-142

"Type 75"

[24]**"LHD"**

defenceforumindia.com

The Chinese navy has announced that it has begun construction of a new class of amphibious vessels. They are to be "LHD's", bigger than the French "Mistral" class and the Spanish "Juan Carlos 1" class.

They will have a displacement of approximately 35,000 tonnes and have dimensions around the same as a "Mistral" class. They will have a full-length flight deck, with five helicopter-landing spots. The stern will have a large docking well, big enough to take "air-cushioned landing craft.

Details about how many helicopters and landing craft it will carry have not yet been announced. Troop numbers and vehicle storage capacity, are also a mystery.

According to reports, the vessel/vessels are being built at the Hudong shipyard, in Shanghai. Just how many of these ships China will build is not known. The vessels, along with the other new amphibious ships, will make Taiwan very nervous.

---

[24] Source http://defenceforumindia.com/forum/threads/china-military-photos-videos.3157/page-91

Tank Landing Ships

"Yukan" class "Type 072"

25"Wufeng Shan"

櫻井千一

Name	Pennant	Completed	Builder
Yuntai Shan	927	1978	Zhonghua
Wufeng Shan	928	1980	Zhonghua
Zijin Shan	929	1982	Zhonghua

Displacement. 3,100 tonnes   **Dimensions.** 120m x 15.3m x 2.9m
Speed. 18 knots   **Complement.** 130
Armament. 4 x twin 57mm guns; 4 x twin 25mm guns

Notes
These three ships are the forerunners to the very successful "Type 072 II & III"
class of landing ships. They were built to replace the old, World War 2 type of
landing ships that were acquired from the US Navy. They were also the first
indigenous built landing ships to be built in China. They are able to transport
and put ashore over a dozen vehicles of various size or 200 troops. 500 tonnes
of cargo can also be carried. The main way of disembarkation is by beaching
the vessels and unloading via the bow doors. All three are assigned to the East
Sea fleet.

"Yuting" class "Type 072 II"

[26]"Liupan Shan"

櫻井千一

Name	Pennant	Completed	Builder
Lingyan Shan	930	1995	Zhonghua
Dongting Shan	931	1995	Zhonghua
Helan Shan	932	1995	Zhonghua
Liupan Shan	933	1995	Zhonghua

Displacement. 3,430 tonnes   **Dimensions.** 119.5m x 16.4m x 2.8m
Speed. 14 knots   **Complement.** 104
Armament. 1 x twin 57mm guns; 3 x twin 37mm guns

Notes
These four vessels are the first of the "Yuting" class. They are also the first "Tank Landing Ships", with a helicopter pad. They are capable of transporting 250 troops and their equipment or 500 tonnes of stores. The vehicle deck is capable of handling over a dozen armoured vehicles of various sizes. The ships are designed to be beached and to unload via the bow doors.
"Lingyan Shan" is assigned to the East Sea fleet, while the other three are with the South Sea fleet.

---

[26] Source https://commons.wikimedia.org/wiki/File:Yuting_class_LST%EF%BC%88Type_072II-class%EF%BC%89_933_Liupanshan.jpg

"Yuting II" class "Type 072 III"

[27]"Xuefeng Shan"   defenceforumindia.com

Name	Pennant	Completed	Builder
Emei Shan	991	1992	Zhonghua
Danxia Shan	934	1995	Zhonghua
Xuefeng Shan	935	1995	Zhonghua
Haiyang Shan	936	1996	Zhonghua
Qingcheng Shan	937	1996	Zhonghua
Luliang Shan	938	1997	Zhonghua
Yandang Shan	908	1997	Zhonghua
Jiuhua Shan	909	2000	Zhonghua
Putuo Shan	939	2000	Zhonghua
Huanggang Shan	910	2001	Zhonghua
Tiantai Shan	940	2002	Zhonghua

Displacement. 3,430 tonnes
Speed. 18 knots
Armament. 3 x twin 37mm guns

Dimensions. 119.5m x 16.4m x 2.8m
Complement. 104

Notes
These eleven ships are an improved design to the "Yuting" class. These vessels have a greater speed and a redesigned superstructure. They are capable of transporting 250 troops and their equipment or 500 tonnes of stores. The

---

[27] Source http://defenceforumindia.com/forum/threads/china-military-photos-videos.3157/page-128

vehicle deck is capable of handling over a dozen armoured vehicles of various sizes. The ships are designed to be beached and to unload via the bow doors. There is a helicopter deck but this has been re-positioned at the stern of the vessels. There is no hangar or support facilities.

"Emei Shan" is based with the South Sea fleet. "Yandang Shan", "Jiuhua Shan" and "Huanggang Shan" are assigned to the North Fleet. All other vessels are with the East Fleet.

[28]"Yandang Shan"

---

[28] Source http://defenceforumindia.com/forum/threads/china-military-photos-videos.3157/page-134

"Yuting III" class "Type 072A"

[29]"Tianzhu Shan"

defenceforumindia.com

Name	Pennant	Completed	Builder
Tianzhu Shan	911	2003	Dalian
Daqing Shan	912	2003	Dalian
Baxian Shan	913	2003	Zhonghua
Huading Shan	992	2003	Wuchang
Luoxiao Shan	993	2004	Zhonghua
Daiyun Shan	994	2004	Wuchang
Wangang Shan	995	2004	Zhonghua
Laotie Shan	996	2005	Dalian
Luhua Shan	997	2004	Wuchang
?	981	2015	?
?	982	?	?
?	983	?	?

Displacement. 3,430 tonnes
Speed. 21 knots
Armament. 1 x twin 37mm guns

Dimensions. 119.5m x 16.4m x 2.8m
Complement. 104

Notes

These vessels are an evolution of the "Type 072 III" class. There are at least nine ships in service, with another three under construction. They are the same displacement and have the same dimensions as the previous class but have internal differences. The vehicle deck has been shortened to allow the installation of a docking well at the stern. This is large enough to take an "Air-cushioned Landing Craft". There is a helicopter pad above the docking well. They are capable of transporting 250 troops and their equipment or 500 tonnes of stores. The vehicle deck is capable of handling almost a dozen armoured vehicles of various sizes. The ships are also designed to be beached and to unload via the bow doors.

"Tianzhu Shan" and "Daqing Shan" are assigned to the Northern fleet. "Baxian Shan" is with the East Sea fleet, while the other vessels are with the South Sea fleet.

[30]"Daiyun Shan" & "Luoxiao Shan"

defenceforumindia.com

Source http://defenceforumindia.com/forum/threads/china-military-photos-videos.3157/page-136

"Yunshu" class "Type 073A"

No Photo available

Name	Pennant	Completed	Builder
Wudang Shan	990	1994	Zhonghua
Sheng Shan	941	2004	Zhonghua
Lu Shan	942	2004	Zhonghua
?	943	2004	Zhonghua
Yu Shan	944	2004	Zhonghua
Hua Shan	945	2004	Zhonghua
Song Shan	946	2004	Zhonghua
?	947	2004	Zhonghua
Xue Shan	948	2004	Zhonghua
Heng Shan	949	2004	Zhonghua
Tai Shan	950	2004	Zhonghua

Displacement. 2,000 tonnes　　**Dimensions.** 87m x 12.6m x 2.25m
Speed. 17 knots　　**Complement.** 70
Armament. 2 x twin 37mm guns

Notes
The first unit of this class was completed approximately ten years before the others. The reason for this may have been problems with the propulsion system. The following ten had much more reliable engines.
They are able to carry 250 tonnes of stores or 500 troops and their equipment. Up to ten armoured vehicles can be carried on the vehicle deck. To unload its cargo, the ship beaches and opens its bow doors.

"Yudao" class "Type 073 IIY"

[31]"Yudao" class

Displacement. 1,460 tonnes
Speed. 17 knots
Armament. 4 x twin 25mm guns

Dimensions. 78m x 12.6m x 3.1m
Complement. 65

Notes

In 1985, two vessels were built to a modified design of the "Type 073" class. As the construction plans for a large class had been abandoned because of an unreliable engine design, only two units were built. As only one each of the preceding "Type 073" and "Type 073 II" were built, it can be assumed that the perfection of this design has been a "labour of love".

Source http://defenceforumindia.com/forum/threads/china-military-photos-videos.3157/page-30

"Yuhai" class "Type 074"

[32]"7593"

Tkstevens

Name	Pennant	Completed	Builder
	3111	1995/2000	Wuhu Shipyard
	3113	1995/2000	Wuhu Shipyard
	3115	1995/2000	Wuhu Shipyard
	3116	1995/2000	Wuhu Shipyard
	3117	1995/2000	Wuhu Shipyard
	3229	1995/2000	Wuhu Shipyard
	3244	1995/2000	Wuhu Shipyard
	7593	1995/2000	Wuhu Shipyard
	7594	1995/2000	Wuhu Shipyard
	7595	1995/2000	Wuhu Shipyard
	3128	2005/2007	Wuhu Shipyard
	3129	2005/2007	Wuhu Shipyard
	3232	2005/2007	Wuhu Shipyard
	3233	2005/2007	Wuhu Shipyard
	3234	2005/2007	Wuhu Shipyard
	3235	2005/2007	Wuhu Shipyard

Displacement. 800 tonnes
Speed. 18 knots
Armament. 3 x twin 25mm guns

Dimensions. 58.4m x 10.4m x 2.7m
Complement. 56

---

[32] Source
https://commons.wikimedia.org/wiki/File:%E9%A7%90%E6%B8%AF%E9%83%A8%E9%9A%8A%E8%89%A6%E8%89%87%E5%A4%A7%E9%9A%8A_-_7593%E7%99%BB%E9%99%B8%E8%89%87.JPG

Notes

These small "Tank Landing Ships" have been designed and built, drawing on experience gained from previous ship classes. They are capable of operating at sea but not in extreme weather.

They are able to carry up to 100 tonnes of equipment. Alternatively, they can accommodate two main battle Tanks or six other lighter vehicles on the vehicle deck. 350 troops can also be embarked. To disembark its cargo, the vessels beach themselves and unload via the bow doors.

The last six vessels were built to a slightly modified design. The only change on the outside is the 2 twin 14mm guns, as opposed to the 3 twin 25mm guns.

Landing Craft

"Yunnan" class "Type 067"

[33]"Yunnan" class   unknown

Displacement. 135 tonnes   **Dimensions.** 28.6m x 5.4m x 1.5m
Speed. 12 knots   **Complement.** 12
Armament. 2 x twin 25mm or 14.5mm guns

Notes
Approximately, 130 of these landing craft were built between 1968 and 1972.
Many were for the Sri Lankan and Cameroon navies. They are able to carry 46
tonnes of equipment or the same weight of vehicles. Most have stayed in
Chinese service. Many were converted to be used as cable layers or buoy
tenders.

"Zubr" class

[34]"Zubr" being delivered

defenceforumindia.com

Name	Pennant	Completed	Builder
		2011	Ukraine Shipyard
		2012	Ukraine Shipyard
		2012?	China Shipyard
		2012?	China Shipyard

Displacement. 340 tonnes
Speed. 63 knots
Armament. 2 x 30mm AK-630 guns

Dimensions. 57m x 25.6m x 1.6m
Complement. 31

Notes
These were the biggest military hovercraft ever built and are relics of the Cold War. They were designed and built in the Soviet Union just before the end of the Cold War. Their design was influenced by the Soviet "bigger was better" principle. There are almost a dozen in service with the Russian Navy, the Ukraine navy and now Chinese. Greece acquired four vessels but have recently sold them. China placed an order for four vessels in 2009 and they were all in service by 2012, according to reports. Two were built in the Ukraine and two in China. They can carry 150 tonnes of vehicles or stores or 500 troops and their equipment.

---

[34] Source http://defenceforumindia.com/forum/threads/china-military-photos-videos.3157/page-144

"LCAC" "Type 726"

³⁵"3157"

Displacement. 150 tonnes
Speed. 40 knots

Dimensions. 30m x 16m x m
Complement. 7

Notes

This type of landing craft began to be developed in the late 1960s. It was not until 1978 that an "LCAC", "Type 716" was built at the Hudong Shipyard because of the political situation. This type did not enter production because of technical failures. A second design however, was already in the pipeline. The "Type 722", was heavier and had bow and stern ramps plus it could carry a heavier payload. The first production model entered service in 1979 and it is believed that there are approximately ten still in service. In 1989, an improved "Type 722 II", entered service. This was slightly heavier and could carry a payload of twenty tonnes compared to fifteen of the earlier type. These were built in small numbers, with no confirmed word on how many are still in service. In 2009, a new design was launched at the Jiangnan Shipyard, named the "Yuri" class. This was the "Type 726", which is most commonly seen. It is considered to be the equivalent of the American "LCAC". The Chinese version however, carries less of a load because of inferior engine design. It can still

---

35
Source http://defenceforumindia.com/forum/threads/china-military-photos-videos.3157/page-134

carry 60 tonnes, which is one main battle tank or lighter vehicles. The Chinese are obviously very happy with the design, as they have built the "Yuzhoa" class, Amphibious Assault ships, to be able to accommodate four "Type 726" LCAC. It is believed that at least 30 "Type 726's" have been built and are in service. It is expected that the Chinese will build more of these "LCAC's" as they expand their amphibious fleet.

[36]"LCAC 3320"

defenceforumindia.com

36
Source http://defenceforumindia.com/forum/threads/china-military-photos-videos.3157/page-134

"LCAC" "Type 724"

[37] "Type 724"

defenceforumindia.com

Displacement. 6.5 tonnes
Speed. 40 knots

Dimensions. 12.4m x 4.7m x m
Complement. 3

Notes

This "Air-cushioned Landing Craft", was designed in the late 1970s/early 1980s. It is an improved design of the "Type 711". The program was delayed by over a decade owing to the "Cultural Revolution" and the following political upheaval. It was not until 1994 that the first example came off the production line. It is estimated that between 20 to 30 craft were built. They are designed to carry personnel and no heavy equipment. One major drawback to the design is that the passenger compartment has no protection, leaving the occupants open to enemy fire. These craft do however; have the ability to land troops in very swampy land and very shallow coastlines.

Destroyers

"Luhu" class "Type 052"

[38]"Harbin"

defenceforumindia.com

Name	Pennant	Completed	Builder
Harbin	112	1994	Jiangnan Shipyard
Qingdao	113	1994	Jiangnan Shipyard

Displacement. 4,800 tonnes   **Dimensions.** 144m x 16.5m x 5.1m
Speed. 31 knots   **Complement.** 260
Armament. 1 x 100mm gun; 2 x 30mm CIWS guns; 16 YJ-83 SSM
         1 x 8 cell HQ-7 SAM; 2 x triple 324mm torpedo tubes
         2 x 6 barrel anti-submarine rocket launchers
Aircraft. 2 x ASW Helicopters

Notes
These two vessels were China's first attempt at designing and building multi-role vessels. Most of the weapon systems, sensors and radars are of foreign origin. This supply of foreign equipment had helped the Chinese fill gaps in their shipbuilding industry for a number of years but this all stopped in 1989, after the "Tiananmen Square" massacre.

---

[38] Source http://defenceforumindia.com/forum/threads/china-military-photos-videos.3157/page-101

Even though these ships are very well armed and have a good balance of weaponry, much of it was added without many of the systems being compatible. Many commentators believed that these ships were experimental. After completion, each ship had a different weapon suite with many foreign and "home grown", Chinese systems. Only after refits and modernisations have they acquired the same weaponry.

Both vessels are assigned to the North Sea fleet.

[39]"Qingdao"

defenceforumindia.com

---

[39] Source http://defenceforumindia.com/forum/threads/china-military-photos-videos.3157/page-134

"Luyang" class "Type 52 B"

[40]"Guangzhou"

Name	Pennant	Completed	Builder
Guangzhou	168	2004	Jiangnan Shipyard
Wuhan	169	2004	Jiangnan Shipyard

Displacement. 5,850 tonnes **Dimensions.** 155m x 17m x 6m
Speed. 30 knots **Complement.** 280
Armament. 1 x 100mm gun; 2 x 30mm CIWS guns; 16 YJ-83 SSM
2 x SA-N-12 SAM; 2 x triple 324mm torpedo tubes
2 x 12 barrel 240mm anti-submarine rocket launchers
Aircraft. 1 x ASW Helicopter

Notes
These two vessels are the first of the very successful "Luyang" class. Two further class of vessels followed this one, "Luyang II" and "Luyang III".   This class of destroyers were the first Chinese built vessels with a modern, up-to-date surface-to-air capability. They were also the first to incorporate "stealth" features in the hull and superstructure.
They are armed with a well-balanced weapon suite of surface-to-surface, surface-to-air and anti-submarine weaponry. Most of the weapon systems are

[40] Source http://defenceforumindia.com/forum/threads/china-military-photos-videos.3157/page-132

Chinese, apart from the surface-to-air weapons, which are of Russian origin. These destroyers represent China's ambition to build and deploy a "blue water" fleet, which can project power well beyond China's regional waters. Both vessels are assigned to the South Sea fleet.

[41]"Guangzhou" and "Wuhan" foreground

defenceforumindia.com

"Luyang II" class "Type 052C"

[42]"Haikou"

USCG/Manda M.Emery

Name	Pennant	Completed	Builder
Lanzhou	170	2005	Jiangnan
Haikou	171	2005	Jiangnan
Changchun	150	2013	Changxingdao-Jiangnan
Zhengzhou	151	2013	Changxingdao-Jiangnan
Jinan	152	2014	Changxingdao-Jiangnan
Xi'an	153	2015	Changxingdao-Jiangnan

Displacement. 7,000 tonnes   **Dimensions.** 155.5m x 17.2m x 6.1m
Speed. 29 knots   **Complement.** 280
Armament. 1 x 100mm gun; 2 x 30mm CIWS; 2 x triple 324mm torpedo tubes
   8 x C-805 or HN-2 or YJ-62 cruise missiles
   1 x 48 cell VLS HHQ-9 SAM
Aircraft. 1 x ASW helicopter

---

[42] Source https://commons.wikimedia.org/wiki/File:CNS_Haikou_(DDG-171)_in_Rim_of_the_Pacific_(RIMPAC)_Exercise_2014.jpg

Notes

These six vessels are the second "batch", of the "Luyang" class. There was gap of almost a decade between the first two vessels and the next four.

The weapon systems on these ships are a marked improvement of the previous "Luyang" class. Most of the weapons are of Chinese origin but there is still a Russian influence. The most obvious difference is the surface-to-air systems. The old Russian missile launchers have been replaced by a 48 cell "Vertical Launch System". These missiles have a range of approximately 200 kms. They also have a powerful anti-submarine armament, with torpedoes and a "Kamov" or a "Harbin" ASW helicopter. The flight deck is at the stern, with a hangar and support facilities. There is a strong anti-ship missile armament with the cruise missiles embarked.

"Lanzhou" and "Haikou" are assigned to the South Sea fleet while the others are with the East Sea fleet.

[43]"Zhengzhou"

defenceforumindia.com

---

[43] Source http://defenceforumindia.com/forum/threads/china-military-photos-videos.3157/page-147

"Luyang III" "Type 052D"

[44]"Luyang III" class

defenceforumindia.com

Name	Pennant	Completed	Builder
Kunming	172	2014	Jiangnan
Changsha	173	2015	Jiangnan
Heifei	174	2015	Jiangnan
Yinchuan	175	2016	Jiangnan
Xining	117	2016	Jiangnan
Taiyuan	118	Expected 2017	Jiangnan
Xiamen	154	Expected 2017	Jiangnan
?	119	Expected 2017	Dalian Shipyard
Guiyang	155	Expected 2017	Jiangnan
?	120	Expected 2018	Dalian Shipyard
?	156	Expected 2018	
?	157	Expected 2018	

Displacement. 7,000 tonnes **Dimensions.** 156m x 18m x 6.5m
Speed. 30 knots **Complement.** 280
Armament. 1 x 130mm gun; 1 x 30mm CIWS; 2 x 30mm guns
          1 x 64 cell VLS combined SAM & SSM
          1 x HHQ-10 short-range SAM; 2 x triple 324mm Torpedo tubes
Aircraft. 1 x ASW helicopter

Notes

These ships are the third "batch" of the "Luyang" class. Twelve vessels have
been planned with half already in service. The rest are either fitting-out or under
construction. They are an "all-round" improvement from the "Luyang II" class.
These are very powerful ships with the most modern weapon systems that
China, with Russia's help, can offer. The surface-to-surface weaponry has been
increased to a 130mm main gun and more short-range guns. The surface-to-air
systems have been increased with a 64 cell "Vertical Launch System", firing
long-range SAM's. There is also a short-range SAM's comparable to the US
Navy "RAM" system. The anti-ship cruise missiles are housed in the 64 cell
VLS. They also have a powerful anti-submarine armament, with torpedoes and
a "Kamov" or a "Harbin" ASW helicopter. The flight deck is at the stern with a
hangar and support facilities.
All three types of the "Luyang" class represent a great leap forward in China's
capability and ambitions for strong "blue water" fleet.
"Kunming", "Changsha", "Heifei" and "Yinchuan" are based with the South Sea
fleet. "Xining", Taiyuan" and "119" will be based with the North Sea fleet, while
the remaining ships will be with East Sea fleet.

[45]"Kunming"

海防先锋

[45] Source https://commons.wikimedia.org/wiki/File:CNS_Kunming_(DDG-172).jpg

"Luda" class "Type 051"

[46]"Zhunai"

US Navy/Eric Murata

Name	Pennant	Completed	Builder
Nanchang	163	1982	Guangzhou
Kaifeng	109	1982	Dalian
Dalian	110	1984	Zhonghua
Zunyi	134	1984	Dalian
Guilin	164	1987	Guangzhou
Zhanjiang	165	1989	Dalian
Zhuhai	166	1991	Dalian

Displacement. 3,670 tonnes   **Dimensions.** 132m x 12.8m x 4.6m
Speed. 32 knots   **Complement.** 280
Armament. 2 x twin 130mm guns; 4 x twin 37mm guns
               2 x triple 324mm torpedo tubes; 16 x YJ-83 SSM
               1 x 8 cell HQ-7 SAM; 2 x Anti-submarine rocket launchers

Notes

This class of destroyer was the first "Guided Missile Destroyers" to be designed
and built in China. Their design is based on the Soviet "Kotlin" class destroyer.
They have been optimized for surface-to-surface combat. They do have
surface-to-air missile but these are short-range, point-defence weapons. There
were originally 17 vessels in this class but most have been decommissioned
and given other roles.
The vessels, which are still active, were given mid-life modernisations just after
the turn of the century. This has enabled them to operate until the end of this
decade.

---

[46] Source https://commons.wikimedia.org/wiki/File:Luda-III_Zhuhai_DN-SD-01-05827.jpg

"Jinan" was commissioned in 1971 and decommissioned in 2007. "Yinchuan" and "Nanjing" were commissioned in 1976 and 1977 respectively and both decommissioned in 2012. "Xining" was commissioned in 1980 and decommissioned in 2013. All four ships have been converted to museum ships. "Xi'an" was commissioned in1974 and decommissioned in 2007. "Hefei" was commissioned in 1980 and decommissioned in 2012. "Changsha" was commissioned in 1975 and decommissioned in2008. All three ships have been laid-up and are used as training vessels.

"Guangzhou" was commissioned in 1977 and sank in 1978 due to an explosion. "Nanning" and "Chongqing" were decommissioned in 2012 and 2014, respectively.

"Nanchang", "Guilin", "Zhanjiang" and "Zhuhai" are with the South Sea fleet. "Zunyi" is with the East Sea fleet. "Dalian" and "Kaifeng" are both with the North Sea fleet.

[47]"Zhunai"

US Navy

"Luhai" class "Type 051 B"

[48] "Shenzhen"   US Navy/Nathanael T. Miller

Name	Pennant	Completed	Builder
Shenzhen	167	1999	Dalian

Displacement. 6,100 tonnes   **Dimensions.** 153m x 16.5m x 6m
Speed. 31 knots   **Complement.** 250
Armament. 1 x 100mm gun; 4 x twin 37mm guns
             2 x triple 324mm torpedo tubes; 16 x YJ-83 SSM
             1 x 8 cell HQ-7 SAM; 2 x Anti-submarine rocket launchers
Aircraft. 2 x ASW helicopters.

Notes
When this ship was constructed, she was the largest surface warship designed
and built in China. She was also the first Chinese vessel to have a sloping
superstructure to reduce her radar signature.
"Shenzhen" is, basically, an experimental vessel. Only one ship has been built,
to gain experience in designing and building large, modern vessels. When she
was completed, it was a surprise to see that her surface-to-air weaponry was
the older "HQ-7" system. Her anti-submarine armament is very strong, with two
anti-submarine helicopters, plus hangar facilities and triple torpedo launchers.

---

[48] Source https://commons.wikimedia.org/wiki/File:Shenzhen_(DDG_167).jpg

In 2015, she was spotted in dry-dock at the Zangjiang naval base, midway through, what looked like, a major refit. All of her armament had been removed, along with radar and sensors. When she emerges, she will probably have a "Vertical Launch System", SAM "30mm CIWS", were already shown, in place of the "37mm" guns.

Nevertheless, she has and will be a powerful destroyer with a good balance of surface-to-surface, surface-to-air and anti-submarine weaponry.

She has been assigned to the South Sea fleet and will probably re-join it after her refit.

[49] "Shenzhen"

US Navy/Nathanael T. Miller

---

[49] Source https://commons.wikimedia.org/wiki/File:Chinese_destroyer_Shenzhen_DDG167.jpg

"Luzhou" class "Type 051 C"

[50]"Shenyang"

Name	Pennant	Completed	Builder
Shenyang	115	2006	Dalian
Shijiazhuang	116	2007	Dalian

Displacement. 7,100 tonnes
Speed. 30 knots
Armament. 1 x 100mm gun; 2 x 30mm CIWS
2 x triple 324mm torpedo tubes; 8 x YJ-83 SSM
8 x 6 cell VLS SA-N-20 SAM

Dimensions. 155m x 17m x 6m
Complement. Approx 250

Notes
These two ships are equipped to provide long-range air-defence. Their design is based on the "Luhai" class and is equipped with the advanced "S-300", Russian, missile system. These vessels are not as advanced as other Chinese vessels in terms of hull design and machinery.
These ships do have a very powerful surface-to-surface and surface-to-air armament but the anti-submarine armament is very limited. They are equipped with anti-submarine torpedoes but there is no embarked helicopter. There is a flight deck, at the stern of the vessels but no hangar or support facilities provided. At a quick glance, there does appear to be a hangar but a closer look reveals four of the six "Vertical Launch" cells are positioned there.

It appears that these ships were built as a "stop-gap" measure to provide adequate air-defence ships until newer designs were available. China does have the ability to build ships as experiments whereas the West cannot afford such expenditure and would rather perfect the design on paper or in testing tanks.

Both ships are based with the North Sea fleet.

[51]"Shijiazhuang"

---

[51] Source http://defenceforumindia.com/forum/threads/china-military-photos-videos.3157/page-128

"Sovremenny" class

52"Taizhou"

Astrowikizhang, English language Wikipedia

Name	Pennant	Completed	Builder
Hangzhou	136	1999	Severnaya Verf
Fuzhou	137	2000	Severnaya Verf
Taizhou	138	2006	Severnaya Verf
Ningbo	139	2006	Severnaya Verf

Displacement. 6,600 tonnes   **Dimensions.** 156m x 17.3m x 6.5m
Speed. 32 knots   **Complement.** 296
Armament. 8 x SS-N-22 SSM; 2 x single SA-N-7 medium range SAM;
         2 x twin 130mm gun;
         4 x 30mm multi-barrelled CIWS; 2 x twin 533mm torpedo tubes;
         2 x 6 barrelled ASW mortar
Aircraft. 1 x ASW helicopters

Notes
Seventeen Sovremennys" were built for the Soviet/Russian Navy. They were part of the balanced fleet program and built in parallel to the "Udaloy" class destroyers. The "Sovremennys" were equipped for surface-to-air and surface-to-surface actions whereas the "Udaloy" was primarily an anti-submarine vessel.

---

[52] Source https://commons.wikimedia.org/wiki/File:Taizhou2005Sankt-peterburg.jpg

Construction of the lead ship began in 1976, with two additional ships sold to China during construction. A further two improved ships were later ordered by China and continue in service. These two vessels are the third sub-class of these vessels. They have a different weapon suite than earlier ships. The aft, twin "130mm" gun has been removed and all four of the 230mm AK-630" CIWS have been replaced by the "Kashtan" CIWS.

As with all Soviet/Russian warships, these vessels bristle with armaments and do look very impressive. Unlike earlier Soviet vessels, these ships were designed with the intention of the whole ship being a weapon system and not just adding a gun or missile "here or there", if it fits.

Only five ships remain in service with the Russian Navy with the rest decommissioned or scrapped, owing to lack of funds. It is likely that these five vessels will 'soldier on' until the end of the decade and then be replaced by a planned new twelve-ship class known as "Leader".

From mid-2014, the four Chinese vessels will be in a refit cycle, being modernised to enable them to stay active well into the next decade. Since entering Chinese service, all four have been based with the East Sea fleet.

[53]"Hangzhou"

defenceforumindia.com

"Type 055"

[54]"Type 055"

果壳军事

Name	Pennant	Completed	Builder
	100?	Expected 2018?	Changxingdao-Jiangnan
	101?	Expected 2019?	Dalian

Displacement. 10,000+ tonnes   **Dimensions.** 190m x m x m
Speed. 30 knots   **Complement.** ?
Armament. 1 x 130mm gun; 1 x 30mm CIWS; 1 x 24 cell VLS HQ-10 SAM
          2 x 64 cell VLS for surface-to-air, surface-to-surface,
          anti-submarine missile and cruise missiles.
Aircraft. 2 x ASW helicopters

Notes
A new class of destroyer began construction in 2014. It is known as "Type 055" and it will be the most heavily armed destroyer China has ever built. Not all the weapon suite has been disclosed but it looks as if it will match the South Korean, "Sejong the Great" class, for weaponry. Some reports suggest that it would be the first Chinese ship to deploy weapon calibre lasers and an "electromagnetic rail gun". The "Type 055", will be about the same displacement and dimension size as the "Leader" class, which Russia is developing. This will make these vessels truly cruiser sized.
Reports say the first began construction in 2014, with the second ship ordered soon after. How many China will build remains to be seen. The Chinese navy obviously intends these vessels to be escorts to the new class of aircraft carriers currently being built.

---

[54]
Source https://commons.wikimedia.org/wiki/File:Type_055_destroyer.jpg

Frigates

"Jiangkai" class "Type 054"

[55]"Wenshou"

櫻井千一

Name	Pennant	Completed	Builder
Ma'anshan	525	2005	Hudong-Zhonghua Shipbuilding
Wenshou	526	2006	Huangpu Shipyard

Displacement. 3,900+ tonnes   **Dimensions.** 134m x 16m x 5m
Speed. 27 knots   **Complement.** 165
Armament. 1 x 100mm gun; 4 x 30mm AK-630 CIWS
         8 x YJ-83 SSM; 1 x 8 cell HQ-7 SAM
         2 x triple 324mm torpedo tubes
Aircraft. 1 x ASW helicopter

Notes

These two multi-role frigates entered service in the middle of the last decade. They are the forerunners to the "Jiangkai II" class. Only two were built before construction switched.

These are well-armed vessels, capable of handling any threat in the air and sub-surface. The "YJ-83" SSM's give them a powerful surface punch and the ship-borne torpedo tubes plus the ASW helicopter give them a good anti-

---

[55] Source https://commons.wikimedia.org/wiki/File:Type_054_frigate.png

submarine suite. The surface-to-air systems are good for local and close-in defence.

The weapon suite has a large French influence. Even though the weapons are of Chinese origin, they and the fire control are based on earlier French equipment.

Both vessels are assigned to the East Sea fleet.

[56] "Wenshou"

櫻井千一

---
[56] Source https://commons.wikimedia.org/wiki/File:Type_054_frigate_526_Wenzhou.png?uselang=en-gb

"Jiangkai II" class "Type 054A"

[57]"Yan Cheng"

Name	Pennant	Completed	Builder
Zhou Shan	529	2008	Hudong Shipbuilding
Xu Zhou	530	2008	Huangpu Shipyard
Heng Yang	568	2008	Hudong Shipbuilding
Huang Shan	570	2008	Huangpu Shipyard
Yu Lin	569	2010	Hudong Shipbuilding
Yun Cheng	571	2010	Huangpu Shipyard
Yi Yang	548	2010	Huangpu Shipyard
Chang Zhou	549	2011	Hudong Shipbuilding
Yan Tai	538	2011	Huangpu Shipyard
Yan Cheng	546	2012	Hudong Shipbuilding
Heng Shui	572	2012	Huangpu Shipyard
Liu Zhou	573	2012	Hudong Shipbuilding
Lin Yi	547	2012	Huangpu Shipyard
Wei Fang	550	2013	Hudong Shipbuilding
San Ya	574	2013	Hudong Shipbuilding
Yue Yang	575	2013	Huangpu Shipyard
Da Qing	576	2015	Huangpu Shipyard
Huang Gang	577	2015	Hudong Shipbuilding
Yang Zhou	578	2015	Hudong Shipbuilding
Han Dan	579	2015	Huangpu Shipyard

---

[57] Source http://defenceforumindia.com/forum/threads/china-military-photos-videos.3157/page-147

Displacement. 4,053 tonnes   **Dimensions.** 134.1m x 16m x 5m
Speed. 27 knots   **Complement.** Approx 165
Armament. 1 x 76mm gun; 2 x 30mm CIWS; 8 x C-803 SSM
        1 x 32 cell VLS HQ-16 SAM; 2 x triple 324mm Torpedo tubes
        2 x 6 tube 240mm anti-submarine rocket launchers
Aircraft. 1 x ASW helicopter

Notes
This large class of frigates is far from completion. Twenty have so far been
completed with another four reported to be on slipways. These vessels have the
same hull characteristics as the "Jiangkai" class but they are equipped with
updated weapon systems. Gone is the "HQ-7" SAM, having been replaced with
a state-of-the-art "Vertical Launch System". This is armed with the long-range
"HQ-16" SAM. The four, "30mm AK-630" guns have been replaced by two of the
newer "Type 730" CIWS. The "100mm" gun has been replaced by a "76mm"
gun, which has higher rate of fire.
There is an overall improvement in electronics, sensors and radars, compared
to the "Jiangkai" class. Maintenance periods have been reduced because of an
"inventory system", which automatically informs shore-based facilities on
problems and parts required when the vessel returns to port.
"Yan Tai", "Yan Cheng", "Lin Yi", "Wei Fang", "Da Qing" and "Han Dan" are
assigned to the North Sea fleet. "Zhou Shan", "Xu Zhou", "Yi Yang", "Chang
Zhou", "Huang Gang" and "Yang Zhou" are with the East Sea fleet. The rest are
with the South Sea fleet.

[58]"Yi Yang"   defenceforumindia.com

Source http://defenceforumindia.com/forum/threads/china-military-photos-videos.3157/page-101

"Jianghu" class "Type 053"

[59]"Shaoguan"

defenceforumindia.com

Name	Pennant	Completed	Builder
Taizhou	533	1982	Hudong Shipbuilding
Jinhoa	534	1982	Hudong Shipbuilding
Dandong	543	1985	Hudong Shipbuilding
Shaoguan	553	1985	Hudong Shipbuilding
Zhaotong	555	1987	Hudong Shipbuilding
Linfen	545	1987	Hudong Shipbuilding
Cangzhou	537	1990	Hudong Shipbuilding
Beihai	558	1993	Huangpu Shipyard
Dongguan	560	1993	Huangpu Shipyard
Shantou	561	1993	Huangpu Shipyard
Foshan	559	1994	Huangpu Shipyard
Jiangmen	562	1994	Huangpu Shipyard
Zhoaqing	563	1994	Huangpu Shipyard

---

[59] Source http://defenceforumindia.com/forum/threads/china-military-photos-videos.3157/page-128

Displacement. 1,700+ tonnes   **Dimensions.** 103.2m x 10.2m x 3m
Speed. 26 knots   **Complement.** 190
Armament. 2 x 100mm gun; 4 x twin 37mm guns
            6 x SY-1 SSM; 2 x ASW rocket launchers
            2 x 5 tube ASW mortars

Notes
It is thought that a maximum of 35 vessels of this type were built for the Chinese
Navy between the early 1970s and the mid-1990s. Another 18 were built for
export. Egypt and Burma purchased two each, Thailand purchased four and
Bangladesh bought three. The other seven went to other countries.
Most of the Chinese vessels have been modernised over the years, with the
weapon suite changed from the original armament. The old obsolete, ship-to-
ship missiles have been removed and replaced by more modern "YJ-8" or "YJ-
82" SSM's.
"Beihai" onward were built to a slightly improved design and are sometimes
referred to as a separate class.
The class is old, obsolete, being decommissioned and replaced by newer
vessels, which are coming off the slipways. Some vessels listed here may have
been decommissioned by the time this book is published.

[60]"Type 053's"

defenceforumindia.com

Source http://defenceforumindia.com/forum/threads/china-military-photos-videos.3157/page-16

"Jiangwei I" class "Type 053 H2G"

[61]"Huainan"

Allied Navy

Name	Pennant	Completed	Builder
Tongling	542	1994	Hudong Shipbuilding

Displacement. 2,250 tonnes **Dimensions.** 112m x 12.4m x 4 3m
Speed. 28 knots **Complement.** 168
Armament. 1 x twin 100mm gun; 4 x twin 37mm guns
6 x YJ-83 SSM; 2 x 6 tube ASW rocket launchers
6 x torpedo tubes
Aircraft. 1 x ASW helicopter

Notes
This class of frigate is a great improvement from the "Jianghu" class. They were built with a more balanced and advanced weapon suite. They were also equipped with a helicopter and support facilities.
Four were built before construction switched to the "Jiangwei II" class. "Anqing" and "Huainan" were commissioned in 1992. "Huaibei" was commissioned in 1993. All three were decommissioned in 2015 and transferred to the Chinese Coast Guard. It is very likely that "Tongling" will be decommissioned in 2016 and also go to the Coast Guard.

"Jianwei II" class "Type 053 H3"

[62]"Jiaxing"

SteKrueBe

Name	Pennant	Completed	Builder
Lianyungang	522	1998	Hudong Shipbuilding
Jiaxing	521	1999	Hudong Shipbuilding
Putian	523	1999	Hudong Shipbuilding
Yichang	564	1999	Guangzhou
Huludao	565	2000	Guangzhou
Sanming	524	2000	Guangzhou?
Xiangyang	567	2002	Guangzhou
Huaihua	566	2002	Guangzhou
Luoyang	527	2005	Hudong Shipbuilding
Mianyang	528	2005	Huangpu Shipyard

Displacement. 2,250 tonnes
Speed. 28 knots

Dimensions. 112m x 12.4m x 4 3m
Complement. 168

---

[62] Source https://commons.wikimedia.org/wiki/File:Jiaxing1.jpg

Armament. 1 x twin 100mm gun; 4 x twin 37mm guns
8 x YJ-83 SSM; 2 x 6 tube ASW rocket launchers
6 x torpedo tubes
Aircraft. 1 x ASW helicopter

Notes

This class of frigate is the improved version of the "Jiangwei I" class. It was built in substantial numbers and has proved to be a useful ship-class. They were designed in the late 1980s to replace earlier versions of the "Jianghu" class. The most obvious improvements are the 8-cell "HQ-7" SAM system and the 8 "YJ-83" SSM's.

"Yichang", "Huludao", "Sanming", "Xiangyang" and "Huaihua" all serve with the South Sea fleet. "Lianyungang", "Jiaxing" and "Putian" are with the East Sea fleet. "Luoyang" and "Mianyang" are with the North Sea fleet.

[63]"Sanming"

日本防衛省·統合幕僚監部

---

63 Source https://translate.google.co.uk/translate?hl=en&sl=zh-CN&u=https://commons.wikimedia.org/wiki/Category:Type_053H3_frigate&prev=search

Corvettes

"Jiangdao" class "Type 056"

[64]"Jiangdao" class

樱井千一

Name	Pennant	Completed	Builder
Bengbu	582	2013	Hudong-Zhonghua Shipbuilding
Huizhou	596	2013	Huangpu Shipyard
Meizhou	584	2013	Wuchang Shipyard
Datong	580	2013	Hudong-Zhonghua Shipbuilding
Shangrao	583	2013	Hudong-Zhonghua Shipbuilding
Qinzhou	597	2013	Huangpu Shipyard
Baise	585	2013	Hudong-Zhonghua Shipbuilding
Yingkou	581	2013	Liaonan Shipyard
Jieyang	587	2014	Hudong-Zhonghua Shipbuilding
Ji'an	586	2014	Hudong-Zhonghua Shipbuilding
Qingyuan	589	2014	Huangpu Shipyard
Quanzhou	588	2014	Hudong-Zhonghua Shipbuilding
Luzhou	592	2014	Wuchang Shipyard
Weihai	590	2014	Liaonan Shipyard
Fu Shun	591	2014	Hudong-Zhonghua Shipbuilding
Zhouzhou	594	2014	Hudong-Zhonghua Shipbuilding
Chaozhou	595	2014	Huangpu Shipyard
Sanmenxia	593	2014	Wuchang Shipyard

---

[64] Source https://commons.wikimedia.org/wiki/File:Type_056_corvette_%EF%BC%9F.jpg?uselang=en-gb

Name	Pennant	Completed	Builder
Xinyang	501	2015	Liaonan Shipyard
Huangshi	502	2015	Hudong Shipbuilding
?	598	2015	Liaonan Shipyard
?	599	2015	Huangpu Shipyard
Suzhou	503	2015	Wuchang Shipyard
Suqian	504	2015	Wuchang Shipyard
?	505	2016	Wuchang Shipyard
?	512	2016	Wuchang Shipyard

Displacement. 1,300 tonnes   **Dimensions.** 95m x 11.6m x 4 4m
Speed. 25 knots   **Complement.** 78
Armament. 1 x 76mm gun; 2 x 30mm guns
         4 x YJ-83 SSM; 1 x 8 cell FN-3000 SAM
         2 x triple 324mm torpedo tubes

Notes

This class of corvette is being built in very large numbers as part of the Chinese military build-up. Four shipyards are currently producing these vessels. How many China will build is yet to be seen. They are very well armed for ships of this size. The surface-to-surface weaponry consists of a 76mm gun and four ship-to-ship missiles. The surface-to-air armament is for regional or close-in defence. There is a helicopter pad but no hangar and support facilities provided.

[65] "Shangrao"

櫻井千一

---

[65] Source https://commons.wikimedia.org/wiki/File:Type_056_corvette_583_Ganzhou.jpg

Patrol Boats

"Houbei" class "Type 022"

[66]"Type 022"

defenceforumindia.com

Displacement. 224 tonnes **Dimensions.** 42.6m x 12.2m x 1 5m
Speed. 36 knots **Complement.** 12
Armament. 1 x 30mm CIWS; 1 x FLS-1 SAM
8 x C-801/ C-802/ C-803 SSM

Notes
This class of catamaran patrol boats is being built in very large numbers. The first was launched in 2004, at the Hudong-Zhonghua Shipyard in Shanghai. Over eighty vessels are built to date, with no sign in a halt in construction. These boats are classed as "stealth" boats because of their radical design with the hull based on an Australian design. It has wave-piercing hulls to provide a stable platform. Performance in extreme weather though, is still limited. This keeps these boats well within China's regional waters. China is building permanent island "bastions" currently to guard its waters so their patrol areas may be inside these and China's coastline.
The entire vessel's weaponry, apart from the forward "30mm" CIWS, is enclosed within the superstructure to avoid a radar signature.
These boats are a reminder of what the Soviet Union did during the Cold War. They also built up massive fleets of "missile boats" and "torpedo boats", to take on Western naval forces in mass attacks, hoping to overwhelm the opponent.

---

[66] Source http://defenceforumindia.com/forum/threads/china-military-photos-videos.3157/page-101

Experience has shown that boats of this size, regardless of how many there are, do not do well in large naval engagements. They are more suited to operating in "choke points", where limited sea-space limits manoeuvring.

[67]"Type 022"

defenceforumindia.com

67 Source http://defenceforumindia.com/forum/threads/china-military-photos-videos.3157/page-131

"Shanghai III" class "Type 0621"

No Photo available

Displacement. 170 tonnes   **Dimensions.** 41m x 5.3m x 1 8m
Speed. 25 knots   **Complement.** 43
Armament. 2 x twin 37mm guns; 2 x twin 23mm guns.

Notes
The forerunner to this class of gunboat is the "Shanghai" and "Shanghai II"
classes. It is thought that all of these boats have been withdrawn from service.
There are thought to be about seventeen of the "Shanghai III" class still in
service since 1988. These boats are larger and more heavily armed. Most of
these boats are now in reserve or used as training vessels.
These boats performed well on the export market, with a considerable number
going abroad. In fact, more boats were exported than served in the Chinese
navy.

"Hainan" class "Type 037"

[68]"Type 037"   defenceforumindia.com

Displacement. 430 tonnes   **Dimensions.** 58.77m x 7.2m x 2 2m
Speed. 30 knots   **Complement.** 70
Armament. 2 x twin 57mm guns; 2 x twin 25mm guns
          2 x ASW mortars; 4 x RBU-1200 ASW Rocket launchers

Notes
Over 100 of these "sub-chasers" were built between 1964 and 1982. It is
thought that there are over sixty still in commission. They were originally built to
replace the old Soviet "S O-1" class.
Mainly these boats are used for general patrol duties along China's coast and
her vast waterways.
Every year these boats are being withdrawn from service and many have been
passed on to friendly states e.g. North Korea, Myanmar, Egypt, Bangladesh and
Pakistan have all received boats.

"Haiqing" class "Type 037 I"

[69]"Haiqing" class

Displacement. 478 tonnes   **Dimensions.** 62.8m x 7.2m x 2 4m
Speed. 28 knots   **Complement.** 71
Armament. 2 x twin 37mm guns; 2 x twin 14.5mm guns
                    2 x ASW mortars

Notes
This class of "sub-chaser" is the follow-on design of the "Hainan" class. These
vessels have less anti-submarine armament than their predecessor does. The
weaponry is designed more towards basic patrol duties. There were two
variants of this vessel built. The "Type 037 I" was built by Qiuxin shipyard and
the "Type 037 IS", was built by Huangpu Shipyard. Twenty-seven were
completed from 1982 onward and it is assumed that they are all still in
commission.

---

69 Source http://defenceforumindia.com/forum/threads/china-will-provide-six-patrol-ships-to-pakistan-for-cpec-protection.69566/

"Houxin" class "Type 037 IG"

[70]"Type 037IG"   defenceforumindia.com

Displacement. 478 tonnes   **Dimensions.** 62.8m x 7.2m x 2 4m
Speed. 28 knots   **Complement.** 71
Armament. 2 x twin 37mm guns; 2 x twin 14.5mm guns
        4 x C-801/C-802/C-803 SSM

Notes
This class of missile boat is the follow-on design of the "Hainan" class. These are not equipped with anti-submarine weaponry but they are equipped with anti-ship missiles. This class was built between 1991 and 1999 by Quixing and Huangpu shipyard.
It was intended to use these boats, in conjunction with other missile and torpedo boats, to launch large-scale attacks on enemy shipping thus swamping any defence measure the enemy may have.
It is thought that there are about twenty of these boats in service with the Chinese Navy and six, which have been exported to Myanmar.

"Houxin" class "Type 037 II"

[71]"Type 037"

defenceforumindia.com

Name	Pennant	Completed	Builder
Yangjiang	770	1991	Huangpu Shipyard
Shunde	771	1995	Huangpu Shipyard
Nanhai	772	1995	Huangpu Shipyard
Panyu	773	1995	Huangpu Shipyard
Lianjiang	774	2001	Huangpu Shipyard
Xinhui	775	1999	Huangpu Shipyard

Displacement. 542 tonnes   **Dimensions.** 65.4m x 8.4m x 2 4m
Speed. 32 knots   **Complement.** 47
Armament. 1 x twin 37mm guns; 2 x 30mm CIWS
       6 x C-801 SSM

Notes
These six boats make up the "Hong Kong" squadron. Their design is based on an old US designed boat but China built them to its specifications.

Minesweepers

"Wochi" class "Type 081" & "Type 081 A"

[72]"Jingjiang"   Simon Yang

Name	Pennant	Completed	Builder
Zhangjiangang	805	2007	Jiangnan Shipyard
Jingjiang	810	2007	Jiangnan Shipyard
Liuyang	839	2007?	Jiangnan Shipyard
Luxi	840	2007?	Jiangnan Shipyard
Xiaoyi	841	2012	Jiangnan Shipyard
Taishan	842	2012	Jiangnan Shipyard
Changshu	843	2013	Jiangnan Shipyard
Heshan	844	2013	Jiangnan Shipyard
Qingzhou	845	2014	Jiangnan Shipyard
Yucheng	846	2014?	Jiangnan Shipyard

Displacement. 600 tonnes
Speed. ? knots
Armament. 1 x twin 37mm gun

Dimensions. 65m x 9.3m x 2 6m
Complement. ?

---

[72] Source https://commons.wikimedia.org/wiki/File:Type_081_batch_I_minesweeper.jpg

Notes
These minesweepers are the latest designed by China. They can hunt mines by acoustic and magnetic techniques. The first four vessels are "Type 081". Approximately five years after they were commissioned, a second "batch was completed, known as "Type 081 A".

[73]"Yucheng"

Simon Yang

[73] Source https://commons.wikimedia.org/wiki/Category:PLANS_Yucheng_(MHS-846)#/media/File:Type_081_batch_II_minesweeper_846_attached_to_North_sea_fleet_11th_minesweeper_flotilla_(22204831709).jpg

"Wusao" class "Type 082"

No Photo available

Name	Pennant	Completed	Builder
	800	1987	Jiangxin Shipyard
Xiangshan	801	?	Jiangxin Shipyard
	802	?	Jiangxin Shipyard
	803	?	Jiangxin Shipyard
	806	?	Jiangxin Shipyard

Displacement. 320 tonnes
Speed. 15 knots
Armament. 2 x twin 25mm guns

Dimensions. 44.8m x 6.8m x 2 9m
Complement. 28

Notes
This class of minesweeper was built to replace the old "Type 058" and "Type 7102" classes. The "Wusao's" were designed using experience gained from the previous two class of minesweepers. The "Wusao's" were designed in the 1970s but construction did not begin until the mid-1980s because of the "Cultural Revolution". The ships are equipped with acoustic and magnetic mine detection equipment.
Some sources say that there are over a dozen of these vessels in service but there is only proof of five and details about those are sketchy.

"Wozang" class "Type 082 II"

[74]"Kunshan"

Justin Zhuyan*

Name	Pennant	Completed	Builder
Huoqin	804	2005	Qiuxin Shipyard
Kunshan	818	2011	Qinxin Shipyard

Displacement. 575 tonnes
Speed. 15 knots
Armament. 1 x twin 25mm gun

Dimensions. 44.8m x 6.8m x 2 9m
Complement. Approx 30

Notes
This class has taken many years to be designed and built. They are partly built using Fibreglass hulls. Some reports even suggest that they have Fibreglass superstructures. It has been at least six years between each vessel, this may be because Chinese shipbuilders unfamiliarity with fibreglass construction. One definite advantage is the very low magnetic signature of the vessels.
These minesweepers are usually seen with "Type 529" Drones. These can be crewed or remotely operated and t is thought that there are at least three of these in service.

---

[74] Source http://www.shipspotting.com/gallery/photo.php?lid=2390451

Replenishment Ships

"Fuqing" class "Type 905"

[75]"Hongzehu"   US Navy/MCS Johan Chavarro

Name	Pennant	Completed	Builder
Hongzehu	881	1980	Dalian Shipyard
Poyanghu	882	1982	Dalian Shipyard

Displacement. 21,750 tonnes   **Dimensions.** 168.3m x 21.8m x 9 38m
Speed. 18 knots   **Complement.** 130
Armament. 4 x twin 37mm guns
Aircraft. 1 x helicopter

Notes
This class of replenishment ships is designed to assist in the Chinese "ICBM"
program that China was conducting in the South Pacific. Four ships were
constructed with the first two joining the Chinese Navy immediately. The other
two joined the missile program. One has since been sold to a commercial
company and is now a civilian tanker, while the fourth vessel was sold to
Pakistan and is in service with their Navy.
These vessels are able to transport and transfer at sea over ten thousand
tonnes of diesel fuel, one thousand tonnes of light fuel, four hundred tonnes of

---

[75]
Source https://commons.wikimedia.org/wiki/File:The_Chinese_People%27s_Liberation_Army-Navy_Fuqing-class_fleet_oiler_Hongzehu_(AOR_881)_arrives_at_Joint_Base_Pearl_Harbor-Hickam_2.jpg?uselang=en-gb

fresh and drinking water. Fifty tonnes of frozen goods can also be transferred. All of these stores are transferred on six, transfer stations (three on each side). A helicopter is also embarked to aid in the transfer of stores. This has a hangar and support facilities.

[76]"Shenyang" & "Hongzehu"

日本防衛省·統合幕僚監部

---

[76] Source https://commons.wikimedia.org/wiki/File:CNS_Shenyang_(DDG-115),_CNS_Hongzehu_(AO-881).jpg?uselang=en-gb

"Fusu" class "Type 908"

"Nan Sang"

US Navy/ David Mercil

Name	Pennant	Completed	Builder
Qinghaihu	885	1996	Kerson Shipyard Dalian Shipyard

Displacement. 37,000 tonnes **Dimensions.** 188.9m x 25.33m x 10 41m
Speed. 16 knots **Complement.** 125
Armament. 2 x 30mm CIWS guns
Aircraft. 1 x helicopter

Notes

This class of replenishment ship began life in the Soviet Union. Two ships were laid down in the Ukraine for the Soviet Navy. They were to be named the "Komandarn Fedko" class. Not long after construction began, the Cold War ended and the Soviet Union broke apart. These two ships then became the property of the new Ukrainian government. Construction halted as there were no funds for the new Navy. The two ships were then placed on the market to sell abroad.

In 1993, China bought one incomplete hull, which was then towed from the Ukraine to the Dalian Shipyard in China. In 1996, the newly named "Nan Sang" entered service with the navy. Not long after, she was renamed "Qinghaihu". She is able to transport and transfer 23,000 tonnes of diesel fuel, lubricating oils, fresh water and dry stores. A helicopter is also embarked and provided with a hangar and support facilities.

"Qiandaohu" class "Type 903"

[78]"Qiandaohu"

defenceforumindia.com

Name	Pennant	Completed	Builder
Qindaohu	886	2004	Huangpu Shipyard
Weishanhu	887	2004	Hudong-Zhonghua Shipbuilding

Displacement. 20,500 tonnes   **Dimensions.** 178.5m x 24.8m x 8 7m
Speed. 20 knots   **Complement.** 130
Armament. 4 x 37mm guns
Aircraft. 2 x helicopters

Notes

These two replenishment ships are the first indigenous Chinese replenishment ships. They are the first in the "Type 903" class. Two ships were constructed before construction switched to the "Type 903 A".

These ships have been a great asset to the Chinese Navy, allowing them to carry out, truly, 'out of area' operations. So much so that these ships have been seen regularly assisting Chinese ships in the Indian Ocean during anti-piracy patrols. They are able to carry and transfer at sea - diesel fuel, fresh water and dry stores. Two helicopters are permanently embarked to aid in the transfer of stores.

"Qingdaohu" is assigned to the East Sea fleet and "Weishanhu" is with the South Sea fleet.

---

[78]
Source http://defenceforumindia.com/forum/threads/china-military-photos-videos.3157/page-132

"Taihu" class "Type 903 A"

[79]"Chaohu"

kees torn

Name	Pennant	Completed	Builder
Taihu	889	2013	Huangpu Shipyard
Chaohu	890	2013	Hudong-Zhonghua Shipbuilding
Dongpinghu	960	2014	Huangpu Shipyard
Gaoyaohu	966	2014	Huangpu Shipyard
?	963	2015	Hudong-Zhonghua Shipbuilding
?	965	2015	Huangpu Shipyard

Displacement. 23,400 tonnes   **Dimensions.** 178.5m x 24.8m x 8 7m
Speed. 20 knots   **Complement.** 130
Armament. 4 x 37mm guns
Aircraft. 2 x helicopters

Notes
These replenishment ships are the improved "Type 903" design. The only real difference is that the displacement is heavier. Six have been constructed, which is much needed by the navy, as it is expanding its fleet and its area of influence year-by-year.
"Taihu" and "Dongpinghu" are with the North Sea fleet, while "Chaohu" is with the East Sea fleet.

---

[79] Source https://commons.wikimedia.org/wiki/File:PLANS_Chaohu_(AOR-890)_20150130(1).jpg?uselang=en-gb

"Dayun" class "Type 904" "Type 904 A" "Type 904 B"

[80]"Dayun" class

defenceforumindia.com

Name	Pennant	Completed	Builder
Dongtinghu	883	1992	Jianhnan Shipyard
Jingpohu	884	1992	Jianhnan Shipyard
Fuxianhu	888	2007	Jianhnan Shipyard ?
Junshanhu	961	2015	Jianhnan Shipyard ?
Luguhu	962	2015	Jianhnan Shipyard ?
?	?	2016?	Jianhnan Shipyard ?

"Type 904"

Displacement. 10,975 tonnes **Dimensions.** 156.2m x 20.6m x 6 8m
Speed. 22 knots **Complement.** 240
Armament. 4 x 37mm guns; 4 x twin 25mm guns

Notes

"Dongtinghu" and "Jingpohu" are the original "Type 904" ships. They are often referred to as replenishment ships. They are in fact, general stores ships. They do not have the ability to transfer stores at sea. The davits on each side of the vessels are for motor launches and their main purpose is to supply off-shore garrisons with supplies. The motor launches are the main source of transporting goods from ship-to-shore. There is a helicopter pad but no helicopter is embarked.

"Type 904 A"
Displacement. 15,000 tonnes **Dimensions.** 171.1m x 24.8m x 9m
Speed. 22 knots   **Complement.** 240
Armament. 4 x 37mm guns

Notes
Fifteen years after the first "Type 904" was built, one "Type 904 A", ship was constructed, "Fuxian", before an improved design entered production. "Fuxian" is much larger and can carry a more substantial load. The armament has also been reduced.

"Type 904 B"
Displacement. 15,000 tonnes **Dimensions.** 171.1m x 24.8m x 9m
Speed. 22 knots   **Complement.** 240
Armament. 4 x 30mm
Aircraft. 1 x helicopter.

Notes
This is the third variant of the "Type 904's". Two ships are in service, "Junshanhu" and "Luguhu". A third is still under construction. These ships have an updated weapon suite, with four, "30mm" CIWS guns. There is also a helicopter hangar for the transfer of stores.

"Type 901"

No Photo available

Notes
China is in the process of building a class of "Fast Combat Ships", similar to the US Navy's "Supply" class. These vessels will have dimensions close to the US Navy ships and a displacement of almost 50,000 tonnes, fully loaded. They are being built to enhance China's "out-of-area" capability and to support the new class of aircraft carriers, which China is building.
The number of vessels under construction is not known but it is thought that the lead vessel may already have been launched from the Guangzhou Shipyard.
Each vessel will have a speed of approximately 25 knots and will probably be armed with 30mm CIWS. They will be fitted at least five gantries able to transfer liquid and dry stores. Ships on Port & Starboard can be resupplied at once.
There will also be a flight-deck at the stern with a hangar and support facilities for, probably, two helicopters.

Cargo Ships

"Yantai" class

No Photo Available

Displacement. 3,300 tonnes **Dimensions.** 115m x 15.6m x 3m
Speed. 18 knots **Complement.** 100
Armament. 1 x twin 37mm gun

Notes
Three "Tank Landing Ships" of the "Yukan" class, were converted to cargo/ammunition ships. The construction of these vessels was done in Hudong-Zhongua. They are slightly different from the standard "Yukan" class. They have no bow doors and two holds in front of the superstructure and one behind. Two cranes on the foredeck and one at the stern service the holds.

"Hongqi" class "Type 081"

No Photo available

Name	Pennant	Completed	Builder
Bei-Yun	443	1970s	Chinese Shipyard
Bei-Yun	528	1970s	Chinese Shipyard
Dong-Yun	577	1970s	Chinese Shipyard
Dong-Yun	7656	1970s	Chinese Shipyard
Dong-Yun	771	1970s	Chinese Shipyard
Nan-Yun	835	1970s	Chinese Shipyard
Nan-Yun	836	1970s	Chinese Shipyard

Displacement. 1,950 tonnes
Speed. 14 knots
Armament. 2 x twin 25mm guns
Dimensions. 62m x 28m x 4 4m
Complement. 35

Notes
These cargo ships are currently in service with the Chinese Navy. It is thought they all operate in a reserve capacity. They are often employed in coastal and regional activities. Besides cargo, they can also transport passengers. Some sources say that there are seven vessels in this class but others say the two "Nan" ships are part of the "Qiongsha" class.

"Galati" class

No Photo available

Displacement. 5,300 tonnes
Speed. 12.5 knots
Dimensions. 100.6m x 14m x 6 6m
Complement. 50

Notes
These two vessels were built in Romania in the 1970s. They were then delivered to the Chinese navy. They are capable of carrying 3,750 tonnes of cargo and 250 tonnes of fuel oil. They may have been decommissioned by the time this book is published.

"Danlin" class

No Photo available

Name	Pennant	Completed	Builder
Haiyun	794	1960s	Chinese Shipyard
	827	1960s	Chinese Shipyard
	834	1960s	Chinese Shipyard
	835	1960s	Chinese Shipyard
	V	1960s	Chinese Shipyard
	VI	1960s	Chinese Shipyard
	VII	1960s	Chinese Shipyard
Haileng	531	1960s	Chinese Shipyard
Haileng	591	1960s	Chinese Shipyard
Haileng	592	1960s	Chinese Shipyard
Haileng	594	1960s	Chinese Shipyard
Haileng	972	1960s	Chinese Shipyard
Haileng	975	1960s	Chinese Shipyard

Displacement. 1,290 tonnes   **Dimensions.** 60m x 9m x 4m
Speed. 14 knots   **Complement.** 35
Armament. 2 x twin 14.5mm guns; 1 x twin 37mm gun

Notes
Not many details are available about this class of cargo ships. It is thought there are thirteen in service with the Chinese navy. They were built in the 1960s.

"Dandao" class

No Photo available

Displacement. 1,600 tonnes   **Dimensions.** 65.7m x 12.5m x 4m
Speed. 12 knots   **Complement.** 40
Armament. 2 x twin 14.5mm guns; 2 x twin 37mm gun

Notes
Not many details are available about this class of cargo ships. It is thought there are four in service with the Chinese navy. Seven were originally completed but three were refitted as small tankers. They are larger versions of the "Danlin" class and built in the 1970s.

Troop & Cargo Transports

"Qiongsha" class

No Photo available

Name	Pennant	Completed	Builder
Nan-Yun	830	1980	Guangzhou Shipyard
Nan-Yun	831	1980s	Guangzhou Shipyard
Nan-Yun	832	1980s	Guangzhou Shipyard
Nan-Yun	834	1980s	Guangzhou Shipyard
Nan-Yun	835	1980s	Guangzhou Shipyard
Nan-Yun	833	1980s	Guangzhou Shipyard

Displacement. 2,150 tonnes   **Dimensions.** 86m x 13.4m x 3 9m
Speed. 16 knots   **Complement.** 59
Armament. 8 x 14.5mm guns

Notes
These six ships were all built to one design and then converted to perform
separate tasks. Their primary purpose is to re-supply island garrisons in the
South China Sea. It was thought that one design would be able to provide all
the support necessary but this did not work out. There are now three different
types, cargo, troop transport and hospital. The cargo version can carry 200
tonnes of stores and 150 tonnes of fresh water. Two vessels, "Nan-Yun 832" &
"Nan-Yun 833" were converted to hospital ships. Their troop-carrying ability was
removed and replaced with a 130 patient-care facility. They can still carry 350
tonnes of supplies and medical equipment. The troop-carrying version can
accommodate 400 troops and 350 tonnes of cargo. All of the original clinics and
other small departments have been removed to provide extra accommodation
spaces.

"Yuan Wang" class

[81]"Yuan Wang 22"

Vladimir Kynaz*

Name	Pennant	Completed	Builder
Yuan Wang	21	2013	Jiangnan Shipyard
Yuan Wang	22	2014	Jiangnan Shipyard

Displacement. 9,080 tonnes
Speed.

Dimensions. 130m x 19m x 5.9m
Complement.

Notes
These two vessels have been built to participate in China's space program. Even though they are not tracking ships, they are sometimes grouped into the "Yuan Wang" class of tracking ships because of their links to the space program. They are cargo ships, which can transport most of the equipment associated with the program.

81
Source http://www.shipspotting.com/gallery/photo.php?lid=2292459

Coastal Tankers

"Leizhou" class

No Photo available

Displacement. 900 tonnes **Dimensions.** 53m x 9.8m x 3m
Speed. 11 knots **Complement.** 30
Armament. 2 x 14.5mm guns

Notes
Not many details are available about this class of small tankers. It is thought there are nine in service with the Chinese navy but this may have changed by the time this book is published. Four were completed as small water tankers being able to transport 450 tonnes of fresh water. Five were built as oil tankers. All were built in 1960s.

"Shengli" class

No Photo available

Name	Pennant	Completed	Builder
Dong-You	620	1980s	Hudong-Zhonghua Shipbuilding
Dong-You	621	1980s	Hudong-Zhonghua Shipbuilding

Displacement. 4,940 tonnes **Dimensions.** 101m x 13.8m x 5 7m
Speed. 15 knots **Complement.**

Notes
Originally, there were three of these tankers built. It is thought one has been decommissioned, leaving two in the reserve fleet. They are capable of transporting 3,000 tonnes of fuel oil. Both are assigned to the East Sea fleet.

"Fulin" class

[82]"Fulin" class, with different pennant

Bob Godefroy*

Name	Pennant	Completed	Builder
Bei-Shui	572	1970s	Hudong-Zhonghua Shipbuilding
Bei-You	400	1970s	Hudong-Zhonghua Shipbuilding
Bei-You	562	1970s	Hudong-Zhonghua Shipbuilding
Dong-You	632	1970s	Hudong-Zhonghua Shipbuilding
Dong-You	634	1970s	Hudong-Zhonghua Shipbuilding
Dong-You	635	1970s	Hudong-Zhonghua Shipbuilding
Dong-You	638	1970s	Hudong-Zhonghua Shipbuilding
Dong-You	639	1970s	Hudong-Zhonghua Shipbuilding
Dong-You	642	1970s	Hudong-Zhonghua Shipbuilding

---

[82] Source http://www.shipspotting.com/gallery/photo.php?lid=2033475

Name	Pennant	Completed	Builder
Nan-Shu	970	1970s	Hudong-Zhonghua Shipbuilding
Nan-You	961	1970s	Hudong-Zhonghua Shipbuilding
Nan-You	962	1970s	Hudong-Zhonghua Shipbuilding
Nan-You	963	1970s	Hudong-Zhonghua Shipbuilding
Nan-You	969	1970s	Hudong-Zhonghua Shipbuilding

Displacement. 2,200 tonnes   **Dimensions.** 66m x 10m x 4m
Speed. 10 knots   **Complement.** 30

Notes
Twenty of these tankers were built in the 1970s. They are currently being decommissioned and it is thought that these listed are still in service. Many of them have had their pennant numbers changed because of a change in the Chinese naval convention. They are capable of carrying both fuel oil and fresh water.
"Bei-Shu 572", "Bei-You 400" and "Bei-You 562", serve with the North Sea fleet. "Dong-You 632, 634, 635, 638, 639 and 642" are all with the East Sea fleet. "Nan-Shui 970", "Nan-You 961, 962, 963 and 969" are with the South Sea fleet.

[83]"Dong You 632"   Gerolf Drebes*

---

[83] Source http://www.shipspotting.com/gallery/photo.php?lid=1903591

"Fuzhou" class

[84]"Nan-Yun 45"   Brian Fisher*

Name	Pennant	Completed	Builder
Bei-You	560	1960s	Guangzhou Shipyard
Bei-You	563	1960s	Guangzhou Shipyard
Bei-You	573	1960s	Guangzhou Shipyard
Dong-Shui	643	1960s	Guangzhou Shipyard
Dong-Shui	644	1960s	Guangzhou Shipyard
Dong-You	606	1960s	Guangzhou Shipyard
Dong-You	626	1960s	Guangzhou Shipyard
Dong-You	629	1960s	Guangzhou Shipyard
Nan-Shui	938	1960s	Guangzhou Shipyard

---

[84] Source http://www.shipspotting.com/gallery/photo.php?lid=106320

Name	Pennant	Completed	Builder
Nan-You	940	1960	Guangzhou Shipyard
Nan-You	941	1960s	Guangzhou Shipyard

Displacement. 1,200 tonnes   **Dimensions.** 66m x 9m x 3 5m
Speed. 11 knots   **Complement.** 35

Notes
These tankers were built in the late 1960s. They are being decommissioned and it is thought that these listed are still in service. Many of them have had their pennant numbers changed because of a change in the Chinese naval convention. They are capable of carrying both fuel oil and fresh water.
"Bei-You 560, 563 and 573" are with the North Sea fleet. "Dong-Shui 643 and 644" are with the East Sea fleet. "Dong-You 606, 626 and 629" are also with the East Sea fleet. "Nan-Shui 938", "Nan-You 940" and "Nan-You 941" are with the South Sea fleet.

"Type 646"

[85]"Dong-Shui 649", believed decommissioned.

Gerolf Drebes*

Name	Pennant	Completed	Builder
Dong-Shui	646	?	Fujian Shipyard
Dong-Shui	647	?	Fujian Shipyard

Displacement. 670 tonnes
Speed. 10 knots

Dimensions. 38m x 8.2m x 2 3m
Complement. 21

Notes

These two small tankers are designed to carry water and it is believed that they are still in service with the East Sea fleet.

---

[85] Source http://www.shipspotting.com/gallery/photo.php?lid=1907118

"Jinyou" class

[86]Probably not a "Jinyou" class?

Bob Godefroy*

Name	Pennant	Completed	Builder
Dong-Yun	622	1989/90	Kanashashi Shipyard
Dong-Yun	625	1989/90	Kanashashi Shipyard
Dong-Yun	675	1989/90	Kanashashi Shipyard

Displacement. 4,800 tonnes max   **Dimensions.** 99m x 13.8m x 5 7m
Speed. 15 knots   **Complement.** 40

Notes
These tankers were built in Japan during the 1980s. Details about the vessels are hard to come by. The picture shown is probably not a "Jinyou" class tanker as she looks a bit too small.
They are designed to carry fuel oil.

---

86 Source http://www.shipspotting.com/gallery/photo.php?lid=2033478

"Type 631"

[87]"Dong-You 631" and "641"

Gerolf Drebes*

Name	Pennant	Completed	Builder
Bei-You	565	?	?
Dong-You	631	?	?
Dong-You	641	?	?
Nan-You	957	?	?
Nan-You	958	?	?
Nan-You	959	?	?
Nan-You	973	?	?

Displacement. 2,300 tonnes max
Speed. 10 knots

Dimensions. 60m x 10m x 3 3m
Complement. 30

Notes
Details about these vessels are hard to come by. These small tankers are designed to carry fuel oil. "Bei-You", is with the North Sea fleet. Both "Dong-You's ", are with the East Sea fleet. All of the "Nan-You's" are with the South Sea fleet.

87
   Source http://www.shipspotting.com/gallery/photo.php?lid=1903590

Hospital Ships

"Dai san dao hao" class

[88]"Peace Ark"

Chinese defence blog

Name	Pennant	Completed	Builder
Dan san dao hao	866	2008	Guangzhou Shipyard

Displacement. 14,000 tonnes?   **Dimensions.** 178m x 25m x m
Speed. ? knots   **Complement.** ?

Notes
This very large hospital ship is the pride of the Chinese navy's humanitarian force. Very few navies have a dedicated hospital ship and this vessel is certainly one of the best. Details about dimensions and displacement are hard to come by but what is known is that she can handle 300 patients, including 20 intensive care beds and perform 40 major operations per day within her eight operating theatres. This is comparable to a hospital in Beijing.
China states that this vessel was built to allow China to assist in humanitarian missions. Many others believe she was built to aid in China's, "out-of-area" operations.

---

[88]
Source https://commons.wikimedia.org/wiki/File:HS_Peace_Ark-1.jpg

"Zhuanghe" class

No Photo available

Name	Pennant	Completed	Builder
Zhuanghe	865	2004	Seebeckwerft

Displacement. 30,940 tonnes   **Dimensions.** 200.48m x 28.4m x 10m
Speed. 16.7 knots   **Complement.** 32

Notes
This hospital ship is a converted container ship. She is tasked with providing medical evacuation. Her refit to a hospital ship was completed in 2004. The number of containers which she could carry was dramatically reduced and a significant number of rafts and lifeboats were added. No containers are carried above deck anymore to allow for helicopters to land. There are very few details on how many casualties can be accommodated and the number of operating theatres, treatment rooms and ward beds that can be carried. Besides medical duties, "Zhuanghe" can also carry out naval aviation training and troop transport. About 100 container-sized modules are carried below deck for which ever mission is required.

"Beiyi 01" class

No Photo available

Name	Pennant	Completed	Builder
Bei-Yi	01	2010?	?
Dong-Yi	12	2010?	?
Dong-Yi	13	2010?	?
Nan-Yi	10	2010?	?
Nan-Yi	11	2010?	?

These five vessels are classed as naval ambulances. Not much is known of these vessels except there are five in service. It is assumed that they all displace less than one thousand tonnes for them to be classed as "craft". It is known that they are capable of handling helicopters via a flight-deck but there are no hangar facilities.

Multi-role, Aviation Ship

"Shichang" class

No Photo available

Name	Pennant	Completed	Builder
Shichang	82	1997	Quixin Shipyard

Displacement. 9,500 tonnes   **Dimensions.** 125m x 19m x 10.6m
Speed. 17.7 knots   **Complement.** 200

Notes
The "Shichang" was China's first warship, other than destroyers and frigates, to
be able to operate helicopters. She looks almost identical to the British Royal
Navy "Argus" class. "Shichang" however, is smaller. Her main role is training
helicopter pilots and training cadets in general seamanship, with a secondary
role as a casualty evacuation ship. The large weather deck allows containers to
be carried depending on which role she is carrying out.

Training Ship

"Zhenghe" class

[89]"Zhenghe"

Indian Navy

Name	Pennant	Completed	Builder
Zhenghe	81	1983	Jiangnan Shipyard

Displacement. 5,548 tonnes **Dimensions.** 132m x 15.8m x 4.8m
Speed. 17 knots **Complement.** 170
Armament. 2 x twin 57mm guns; 2 x 30mm CIWS

Notes
This is the first training vessel to be designed and built in China. Over forty
different classes can be taught on board by 30 instructors. 170 cadets can also
be accommodated. Most training vessels regularly go on round-the-world
cruises but this vessel completed her first in 2012.

[89] Source
https://commons.wikimedia.org/wiki/File:PLA_Navy_Ships_Zhenghe_and_Weifang_off_Visakhapatnam,_India_in_May_2014.jpg

Barracks Ship

"Xu Xiake" class

No Photo available

Name	Pennant	Completed	Builder
Xu Xiake	88	2011	Guangzhou Shipyard

Displacement. 23,000 tonnes **Dimensions.** 196m x 28m x 8m
Speed. 20 knots **Complement.** ?

Notes
This vessel has been built to support China's Carrier program. Her main task is to accommodate staff working on carrier trails. She is to remain on station, instead of returning to port every night, thus allowing work to continue. The ship can accommodate 2,500 people, for a period of three weeks. When she is not employed on carrier trials, she can be used as a basic training vessel or a troopship.

Icebreakers

"Yanha" class "Type 071"

No Photo available

Name	Pennant	Completed	Builder
Haibing	519	1989	Jiangnan Shipyard

Displacement. 3,200 tonnes   **Dimensions.** 85m x 16m x 5m
Speed. 16 knots   **Complement.**

Notes
Three of these icebreakers have been built. The first and second were commissioned in 1971 and 1973 respectively and have both been decommissioned. The third is still active with the North Sea fleet.

"Yanbing" class "Type 210"

No Photo available

Name	Pennant	Completed	Builder
Haidao	723	1982	?

Displacement. 4,420 tonnes   **Dimensions.** 102m x 17.1m x 5.9m
Speed. 17 knots   **Complement.** 95

Notes
This vessel has been in service since the early 1980s. It was built as an improvement over the previous "Type 071" class. China built has constructed Icebreakers to keep its Northern ports clear of ice. This ship can break ice over one metre thick.
During a modernization, she was fitted with a considerable amount of electronics and intelligence gathering equipment, giving her a secondary, shy-ship role. She is also capable of carrying-out hydrographic surveys of the seabed.

"Type 272"

No Photo available

Name	Pennant	Completed	Builder
Haibing	722	2016	Qiuxin Sipyard

Displacement. 4,480 tonnes   **Dimensions.** 103.1m x 18.4m x 6m
Speed. 18 knots   **Complement.**

Notes
This is the latest Chinese icebreaker to enter service designed and built in
China. She is replacing the previous icebreaker, which had the pennant
"Haibing 722" and is far more capable than her predecessor is. She has a
greater speed and can embark a helicopter. She is to operate in the icy seas of
"Bohai". She will also be employed to carry out search & rescue duties.

Tracking Ships

"YuanWang" class

[90]"Yuan Wang 3"

defenceforumindia.com

Name	Pennant	Completed	Builder
Yuan Wang	3	1995	Jiangnan Shipyard

Displacement. 16,800 tonnes
Speed. 20 knots

Dimensions. 180m x 22.2m x 8m
Complement. 470

Notes
This is the oldest tracking ship in service with the Chinese navy. Details about these vessels are hard to come by. All of the ships of this class differ from each other and are all known as "Yuan Wang". The two previous vessels have both been decommissioned. "Yuan Wang 3", is operated by the "Satellite launch and tracking department" of the Chinese government.

[91]"Yuan Wang 5"   defenceforumindia.com

Name	Pennant	Completed	Builder
Yuan Wang	5	2007	Jiangnan Shipyard
Yuan Wang	6	2008	Jiangnan Shipyard

Displacement. 24,966 tonnes   **Dimensions.** 222.2m x 25.2m x 8m
Speed. 20 knots   **Complement.** 400

Notes
These two tracking ships are in service with the Chinese navy. Details about
these vessels are hard to come by. They are operated by the "Satellite launch
and tracking department" of the Chinese government.

---

91 Source http://defenceforumindia.com/forum/threads/chinas-yuan-wang-class-tracking-ships.14326/

118

Intelligence Ships

"Dondiao" class "Type 815"

[92]"North Star"   defenceforumindia.com

Name	Pennant	Completed	Builder
North Star	851	1999	Hudong-Zhonghua Shipbuilding

Displacement. 6,000 tonnes
Speed. 20 knots
Armament. 1 x twin 37mm gun; 2 x twin 25mm guns
Dimensions. 130m x 16.4m x 6.5m
Complement. 250

Notes
Not long after this ship was completed, she was refitted with three radome's, which replaced her original masts. Aside from general intelligence gathering, this ship is also capable of participating in the Chinese space program.

[92] Source http://defenceforumindia.com/forum/threads/china-military-photos-videos.3157/page-54

"Type 815 A"

93"Tianwangxing"

Name	Pennant	Completed	Builder
Beijixing	851	2010	Hudong Shipbuilding
Tianwangxing	853	2015	Hudong Shipbuilding
Haiwangxing	852	2015	Hudong Shipbuilding
	856	2016	Hudong Shipbuilding

Displacement. 6,000 tonnes **Dimensions.** 130m x 16.4m x 6.5m
Speed. 20 knots **Complement.** 250
Armament. 1 x twin 37mm gun; 2 x twin 25mm guns

Notes

These ships are the improved version of the "Dondiao" class. There is a decade between these two types of ships, with many technical advances. Asides from general intelligence gathering, this ship is also capable of participating in the Chinese space program.

93
Source http://defenceforumindia.com/forum/threads/china-military-photos-videos.3157/page-128

"Bei-Diao" class "Type 814 A"

No Photo available

Name	Pennant	Completed	Builder
Bei-Diao	900	1986	Hudong-Zhonghua Shipbuilding

Displacement. 2,198 tonnes   **Dimensions.** 94.33m x 11.6m x 4m
Speed. 20 knots   **Complement.**

Notes
This ship was part of a Chinese attempt to plug an intelligence gap, which had opened up between China and the West. Four vessels were originally planned and this ship is one of them. Great strides were made in the technical end of the program. Radars, sensors and listening devices were the best that China could produce. She is still in service with the North Sea fleet.

Research Ships

"Xiangyanghong" class "Type 645"

[94]"Xiangyanghong 9"

Kimi2000*

Name	Pennant	Completed	Builder
Xiangyanghong 9	350	1978	Hudong-Zhonghua Shipbuilding

Displacement. 4,435 tonnes
Speed. 19 knots

Dimensions. 112.05m x 15.2m x 5.5m
Complement. 150

Notes
Three vessels of this class were originally built. "Xiangyanghong 14" and "Xiangyanghong 16" were all completed at about the same time as "Xiangyanghong 9" but those two vessels were transferred to civilian service. These ships are equipped with 12 laboratories and have proved to be very useful to the Chinese Navy.

---

[94] Source http://www.shipspotting.com/gallery/photo.php?lid=1569495

"Type 595"

No Photo available

Name	Pennant	Completed	Builder
Xiangyanghong 4	233	1972	Jiangnan Shipbuilding
Xiangyanghong 6	485	1973	Guangzhou Shipbuilding

Displacement. 1,165 tonnes   **Dimensions.** 65.22m x 10.2m x 3.6m
Speed. 15 knots   **Complement.** 82

Notes
These vessels have been in service for over forty years. Three were originally
built but "Xiangyanghong 1", has been decommissioned. These ships were
designed in the 1960s but construction was delayed, as with many projects of
the time, because of the "Cultural Revolution". They were all equipped with an
electric auxiliary power unit to allow less vibration when carrying out sonar
searches. They are being used less and less because of their age.

"Type 625 A & B"

No Photo available

Name	Pennant	Completed	Builder
Haiyang	1	1972	Hudong-Zhonghua Shipbuilding
Haiyang	2	?	Hudong-Zhonghua Shipbuilding
Haiyang	3	?	Hudong-Zhonghua Shipbuilding
Haiyang	4	1980	Hudong-Zhonghua Shipbuilding

Displacement. 2,608 tonnes
Speed. 15 knots
Dimensions. 104.27m x 13.8m x 4.8m
Complement. ?

Notes
Construction of these vessels began in the late 1970s. There was a requirement for four vessels. Three were completed to the "Type A", while the fourth vessel had some improvements and was designated "Type B". The fourth is slightly larger and has more endurance. It is also equipped with much Western scientific equipment.

"Type 625 C"

No Photo available

Name	Pennant	Completed	Builder
Haiyang	11	1981	Hudong-Zhonghua Shipbuilding
Haiyang	12	1981	Hudong-Zhonghua Shipbuilding
Kexue	1	1982	Hudong-Zhonghua Shipbuilding
Shiian	3	?	Hudong-Zhonghua Shipbuilding

Displacement. 3,324 tonnes
Speed. 19 knots
Dimensions. 104m x 14m x 5m
Complement. 38

Notes
These four vessels are an improved design of the "Type A & B" ships. These ships are designated "Type C". They are very much larger than their predecessors are and have a very different internal design. The third and fourth

ships are named differently because of their mix of military and civilian crews. The construction of those two ships also began before "Haiyang 11 & 12". Their construction took longer because of the installation of much more electronic equipment. "Shiian 3" has fourteen laboratories on board, whereas the other vessels are equipped with ten.

"Type 614 i, ii, iii"

No Photo available

Name	Pennant	Completed	Builder
Xiangyanghong	01	1969	Jiangnan Shipyard
Xiangyanghong	02	1972	Guangzhou Shipyard
Xiangyanghong	03	1972	Guangzhou Shipyard
Xiangyanghong	07	1974	Wuhu Shipyard
Xiangyanghong	08	1974	Wuhu Shipyard

"Type 614 i"
Displacement. 1,120 tonnes   **Dimensions.** 66.22m x 10.2m x 3 5m
Speed. 15 knots   **Complement.** ?

Notes
This class of ship was designed in the 1960s. This ship, "Xiangyanghong 01", was required to provide oceanographic studies and also to act as a weather ship. After many years of service with the navy, she was transferred to the Coast Guard where she is still active.

"Type 614 ii, iii"
Displacement. 1,170 tonnes   **Dimensions.** 70m x 10m x 3 4m
Speed. 17.5 knots   **Complement.** ?

Notes
"Xiangyanghong 02 & 03" are an enlarged version of "Xiangyanghong 01" and are "Type 614 ii" ships. They are also used as weather ships and are assigned to the South Sea fleet. Between 1986 and 1988, "Xiangyanghong 03", was refitted to a higher technological standard.
"Xiangyanghong 07 & 08" are "Type 614 iii" ships. They are both dedicated oceanographic survey ships and are assigned to the North Sea fleet.

"Yanlai" class "Type 635"

[95]"Dong-Ce 226"   Gerolf Drebes*

Name	Pennant	Completed	Builder
Bei-Ce	943	1970	Hudong-Zhonghua Shipbuilding
Dong-Ce	227	1972	Hudong-Zhonghua Shipbuilding
Dong-Ce	226	1982	Jiangzhou Shipyard
Nan-Ce	427	1983	Jiangzhou Shipyard
Nan-Ce	420	1975	Guangzhou Shipyard

"Type 635 A, B, C"

Displacement. 1,216 tonnes
Speed. 10 knots

Dimensions. 74.8m x 10m x 3 5m
Complement. ?

Notes
These five ships represent four, slightly different designs. "Bei-Ce 943", is a "Type A" ship and serves with the North Sea fleet. The second ship, "Dong-Ce

---

[95] Source http://www.shipspotting.com/gallery/photo.php?lid=1900079

227", was built to a modified design and is a "Type B" ship. She is with the East Sea fleet. "Dong-Ce 226" and "Nan-Ce 427" are "Type C" ships. They were designed and built using operational experience from the first two vessels. "226" is with the East sea fleet and "427" is with the South sea fleet.

"Type 635 II"

Displacement. 1,245 tonnes **Dimensions.** 81.2m x 9m x 3 5m
Speed. 17 knots **Complement.** ?
Armament. 2 x twin 37mm guns; 2 x twin 25mm guns.

Notes
This vessel, "Nan-Ce 420", is almost different entirely. Not only is she capable of carry out hydrographic surveys but she can also supply submarines and lay mines. She is currently serving with the South sea fleet.

"Type 988"

No Photo available

Name	Pennant	Completed	Builder
Hai-Sheng	582	1972	Guangzhou Shipbuilding

Displacement. 590 tonnes **Dimensions.** 54m x 8.5m x 2.25m
Speed. 15 knots **Complement.**

Notes
Five ships of this class were constructed during the late 1960s and early 1970s. The first four were constructed by Wuchang Shipbuilders and went immediately into civilian service. The fifth vessel however, was built by Guangzhou and was commissioned by the Chinese navy.

"Type 636 A"

[96]"Zhu Kezhen"   Justin Zhuyan*

Name	Pennant	Completed	Builder
Li Siguang	871	1998	Wuhu Shipyard
Zhu Kezhen	872	2004?	Wuhu Shipyard
Qian Sanqiang	873	2015	?

Displacement. 5,883 tonnes   **Dimensions.** 129.28m x 17m x 6m
Speed. 18 knots   **Complement.** 134

Notes
The first ship of this class is a "Type 636". In 2011, she was transferred to the Chinese Coast Guard. The second and third ships are "Type 636 A". Great attention has been paid to anti-vibration measures of these ships. They were originally named "Haiyang 20 and 22", respectively. These names were changed not long after commissioning. They are still in Chinese naval service.

---

[96] Source http://www.shipspotting.com/gallery/photo.php?lid=2365874

Environmental Research Ships

"300 Ton" class

[97]"Dong-Jian 02"   Gerolf Drebes*

Name	Pennant	Completed	Builder
Bei-Jian	10	2007+	?
Dong-Jian	01	2007+	?
Dong-Jian	02	2007+	?
Nan-Jian	01	2007+	?
Nan-Jian	02	2007+	?
Nan-Jian	03	2007+	?

Notes
Details about these vessels are very hard to find. They have been in service for a decade and are known as the "300 ton" class because of their displacement. Their main task is research and sample gathering but they are also used to help larger vessels transfer sewage waste to prevent pollution in the oceans.

[97]
Source http://www.shipspotting.com/gallery/photo.php?lid=1908529

Submarine Repair Ship

"Dadao" class "Type 648"

No Photo available

Name	Pennant	Completed	Builder
Dong-Xiu	911	1985	Bohai Shipyard

Displacement. 1,962 tonnes   **Dimensions.** 84m x 12.4m x 4m
Speed. 15 knots   **Complement.** 105
Armament. 4 x twin 25mm guns

Notes
This ship was part of a program to provide support for a flotilla of submarines.
Two different types of vessel were to have been built. In the end, only this
vessel was built. She can provide maintenance and repair of submarines using
a wide variety of workshops.

Submarine Rescue Ships

"Hudong" class "Type 930"

No Photo available

Name	Pennant	Completed	Builder
Hai-Jiu	512	1969	Hudong-Zhonghua Shipbuilding

Displacement. 2,500 tonnes   **Dimensions.** 85m x 13.5m x 4.19m
Speed. 17 knots   **Complement.**

Notes
This vessel was designed and built in the 1960s because of an incident that
occurred in 1959. A Chinese submarine sank and there was no ship in the
Chinese fleet capable of rendering assistance. The design of this ship is far
from ideal. It does not combine rescue and salvage in one hull so other vessels
have had to be constructed. She is currently based with the East Sea fleet.

"Dazhou" class "Type 946"

No Photo available

Name	Pennant	Completed	Builder
Nan-Jiu	502	1977	Guangzhou Shipbuilders
Bei-Jiu	137	1977	Guangzhou Shipbuilders

Displacement. 1,100 tonnes **Dimensions.** 79m x 9.5m x 2.6m
Speed. 18 knots **Complement.** 130
Armament. 4 x twin 37mm guns; 4 x twin 14.5mm guns

Notes
These two ships were built almost side-by-side. On the same day, six months later, they were launched and handed-over to the Chinese navy. They are equipped to rescue and help salvage downed submarines. "Nan-Jiu" is with the South Sea fleet and "Bei-Jiu", is with the North Sea fleet.

"Dadong" class "Type 946 A"

No Photo available

Name	Pennant	Completed	Builder
Dong-Jiu	304	1982	Hudong-Zhonghua Shipbuilding

Displacement. 1,500 tonnes **Dimensions.** 82m x 11m x 2.7m
Speed. 18 knots **Complement.** 150
Armament. 4 x twin 25mm guns

Notes
This vessel is an enlarged version of the "Type 946". It was the last, single purpose, rescue ship built for the Chinese navy. She is based with the East Sea fleet.

"Dajiang" class "Type 925"

[98]"Yongxingdao"   unknown

Name	Pennant	Completed	Builder
Changxingdao	121	1976	Hudong Shipyard
Chongxingdao	302	?	Hudong Shipyard
Yongxingdao	506	?	Hudong Shipyard
Yongxingdao	863	1985	Hudong Shipyard

Displacement. 10,087 tonnes   **Dimensions.** 156m x 20.6m x 6.8m
Speed. 20 knots   **Complement.** 308
Aircraft. 2 x Helicopters

Notes
These very large vessels are equipped to serve many roles. They can act as a submarine tender and as a rescue and salvage vessel. They are equipped with about every type of ROV and deep submergence vehicle China possesses. The fourth ship was built almost a decade after the first three and has improved systems. She is also heavier, with a displacement of 11,975 tonnes.

"Dalao" class "Type 926"

[99]"Type 926"

defenceforumindia.com

Name	Pennant	Completed	Builder
Oceanic Island	864	2010	Guangzhou Shipyard
Liugong Island	865	2013?	Guangzhou Shipyard
Long Island	867	2013?	Guangzhou Shipyard

Displacement. 9,500 tonnes   **Dimensions.**
Speed.   **Complement.**

Notes
Details about this new class of submarine support ships are hard to come by. It is known that they are the most advanced submarine rescue ships, in service anywhere in the world. This is alongside their capability as a support ship.

---

[99] Source http://defenceforumindia.com/forum/threads/china-military-photos-videos.3157/page-55

Weapon Testing Ships

"Wuhu-B" class "Type 909"

[100]"Bi Sheng"

Simon Yang

Name	Pennant	Completed	Builder
Bi Sheng	891	1997	?

Displacement. 4,630 tonnes
Speed. 18 knots

Dimensions. 129.3m x 17m x m
Complement.

Notes
Not many details are available about this ship because of Chinese secrecy. This vessel is the second such ship to be built for the Chinese navy. It has replaced the "Yanxi" class and is designed to test the latest Chinese missiles and guns. It also tests every new radar, sensor, communication and surveillance system, which is currently under development.

"Dahua" class "Type 909 A"

[101]"Zhan Tianyou"

Simon Yang

Name	Pennant	Completed	Builder
Hua Luogeng	892	2012	?
Zhan Tianyou	893	2012	?
Li Siguang	894	2014	?

Displacement. 4,630 tonnes   **Dimensions.** 129.3m x 17m x m
Speed. 18 knots   **Complement.**

Notes
Not many details are available about this ship because of Chinese secrecy. These vessels are an improved design from the "Type 909" and are designed to test the latest Chinese missiles and guns. They also test every new radar, sensor, communication and surveillance system, which is currently under development. Each ship is able to be refitted with a new system in a very short time to allow testing to commence. Owing to the Chinese naval build-up, it has been necessary to build these vessels to keep up with the vast military development program.

[101] Source https://commons.wikimedia.org/wiki/File:PLA_Navy_underwater_weapon_system_test_ship_893.jpg

Support Ships

Sonar Trials Ship

"Beidiao" class

No Photo available

Name	Pennant	Completed	Builder
Beidiao	993	2000	Jiangxin Shipyard

Displacement. 2,300 tonnes
Speed. 16 knots

Dimensions. 86.4m x 14.6m x 3.8m
Complement. 30

Notes
This is an experimental ship, which has been chartered by the Chinese government and tasked with carrying out tests of sonar and other acoustic equipment. Besides her normal complement, she also has accommodation for up to seventy civilian scientists.

"SWATH" Target Ship

Experiment 216

[102]"Experiment 216"   defenceforumindia.com

This is believed to be a "SWATH", testing platform, which is believed to have entered service in 2014. It has since been converted to a target ship and fitted with radar reflecting equipment and target, simulating electronics. Details are hard to come by, owing to Chinese secrecy.

---

[102] Source http://defenceforumindia.com/forum/threads/china-military-photos-videos.3157/page-130

Torpedo Trials Ships

"Type 906"

No Photo available

Name	Pennant	Completed	Builder
Kancha	3	1987	Hudong-Zhonghua Shipbuilding

Notes
This ship was designed in the early 1980s. The hull is based on the "Type 625" research ship and she is used to test torpedoes, mines and other sub-surface weaponry. In addition, she is also used to test underwater sonar and acoustic electronics. Carrying out hydrographic surveys is another capability.

"Type 907 A"

No Photo available

Name	Pennant	Completed	Builder
Kancha	4	1987	Guijiang Shipyard

Displacement. 615 tonnes
Speed. 15 knots

Dimensions. 52.4m x 8.2m x 2.9m
Complement.

Notes
This vessel is used to carry out experiments and trials of underwater weapons, such as torpedoes, mines, sonars and acoustic detection equipment.

Torpedo Retrieval Ships

"Type 917"

No Photo available

Name	Pennant	Completed	Builder
Bei-Yun	455	1990	Xiamen Shipyard
Bei-Yun	529	1990	Xiamen Shipyard
Nan-Yun	841	1990s	Fujian Mawei Navy Yard
Dong-Yun	803	1998	Guijiang Shipyard
Bei-Yun	484	1998	Guijiang Shipyard
Bei-Yun	485	1999?	Guijiang Shipyard
Dong-Yun	758	2001?	Shanghai Shipyard

Displacement. 720 tonnes
Speed. 13 knots

Dimensions. 63.7m x 9m x 2.8m
Complement.

Notes
These ships are designed to test and retrieve torpedoes. The initial development work of this project began in 1982. Construction of the first and second ships began the following year. It wasn't until 1990 that they were commissioned. This was because the Chinese were still developing the electronic systems and had not perfected the equipment before the ships were built. Once the equipment was ready and installed in the first two ships, more began to be built.
"Bei-Yun 455, 529, 484 and 485", are based with the North Sea fleet. "Dong-Yun 803 and 758", are with the East Sea fleet. "Nan-Yun 841", is with the South Sea fleet.

Diving Tenders

"Kancha" class "Type 904 I & II"

No Photo available

Name	Pennant	Completed	Builder
Kancha	1	1981	Hudong-Zhonghua Shipbuilding
Kancha	2	1983	Hudong-Zhonghua Shipbuilding

"Type 904 I"
Displacement. 1,354 tonnes
Speed. 14 knots

Dimensions. 69.9m x 10.5m x 3.64m
Complement.

"Type 904 II"
Displacement. 1,327 tonnes
Speed. 14 knots

Dimensions. 71.6m x 10.5m x 3.6m
Complement.

Notes
The "Type 904 I" is a modified design of an earlier, proposed ship. The earlier ship was designed with an indigenous diving support system. This unfortunately, did not work so a French system was imported and a new ship designed, which became "Type 904 I". This vessel can support divers to a depth of 200 metres.
The "Type 904 II" is also equipped with a French diving system and is capable of supporting divers to a depth of 300 metres.

Degaussing Ships

"Type 911"

No Photo available

Name	Pennant	Completed	Builder
Nan-Qin	203	1998	Shanghai Shipyard
Dong-Qin	870	2009	Dalian Shipyard

Notes
Technical details about this class of ships is hard to come by. This project was started before the "Cultural Revolution" and has taken this long to build two ships. Chinese technology was way behind the West and it has taken this long for China to catch-up.
Construction of the first vessel did not begin until 1995. Many of the electrical systems are of foreign origin and completely digital. The modern equipment mean that degaussing missions are completed much more quickly than normal. There are plans to build more of these ships but difficulty in developing the necessary equipment is slowing the project.
Both of these ships are based with the East sea fleet.

"Yanbai" class "Type 912"

No Photo available

Name	Pennant	Completed	Builder
Bei-Qin	731	1970	Hudong-Zhonghua Shipbuilding
Nan-Qin	202	1972	Guangzhou Shipyard
Bei-Qin	735	1973	Hudong-Zhonghua Shipbuilding
Dong-Qin	860	?	Guangzhou Shipyard
Dong-Qin	863	1988	Hudong-Zhonghua Shipbuilding
Bei-Qin	736	?	Shengjia Shipyard
Dong-Qin	864	?	Shengjia Shipyard
Nan-Qin	205	?	Shengjia Shipyard

Displacement. 746 tonnes   **Dimensions.** 65m x 8.8m x 2.5m
Speed. 18 knots   **Complement.** 55
Armament. 1 x twin 37mm gun; 2 x twin 14.5mm guns

Notes
Several different types of this ship are in service. All are "Type 912's" but with slight variations. The first two vessels are "Type 912", and these were built following experience with earlier ships. The rest of the class are "Type 912 III's" and have slight differences, such as upgraded electronics and better accommodation.
"Nan-Qin 203" has been retired and replaced by a "Type 911", degaussing ship. It is very likely that by the time this book is published, more of this class will have been decommissioned.
"Bei-Qin 731, 735 and 736", are with the North Sea fleet. "Nan-Qin 202 and 205", are with the South Sea fleet. "Dong-Qin 860, 863 and 864" are with the East Sea fleet.

Rescue/Salvage Ships

"Type 917"

[103]"Dong-Jiu 335"

defenceforumindia.com

Name	Pennant	Completed	Builder
Bei-Jiu	143	2012	Huangpu Shipyard
Dong-Jiu	335	2014	Huangpu Shipyard

Displacement. 650 tonnes
Speed. 30 knots
Armament. 1 x 30mm gun

Dimensions. 78m x m x 2.9m
Complement. 20

Notes
This is the first class of Chinese naval vessel to have a Trimaran hull. This design has enabled the installation of a large flight-deck at the stern for medium to heavy helicopters. It is very possible that the US "Independence" class Trimaran has had an influence in the design of these ships. Two "RIB's" are carried and a 30mm gun. More ships of this class are planned but there is no word on numbers.
"Bei-Jiu 143" is with the North Sea fleet and "Dong-Jiu 335 is with the East Sea fleet.

---

[103] Source http://defenceforumindia.com/forum/threads/china-military-photos-videos.3157/page-146

"Type 922"

No Photo available

Name	Pennant	Completed	Builder
Hai-Jiu	403	1966	Hudong-Zhonghua Shipbuilding
Nan-Jiu	503	1976	Guangzhou Shipyard
Bei-Jiu	122	1987	Wuchang Shipyard
Bei-Jiu	138	1987	?
Dong-Jiu	332	1986	?
Nan-Jiu	510	1986	?

Displacement. 4,450 tonnes   **Dimensions.** 115m x 14.6m x 4.3m
Speed. 20 knots   **Complement.** 200
Armament. 2 x twin 37mm guns; 2 x twin 25mm guns

Notes
These large salvage ships have been built over a protracted length of time. The first ship is the original "Type 922". The following ships are either, "Type 922 II" and "Type 922 III". These ships are slightly different and it is possible that by the time this book is published, the earlier ships will have been decommissioned. "Hai-Jiu 403", "Bei-Jiu 122" and "Bei-Jiu 138", are assigned to the North Sea fleet. "Nan-Jiu 503" and "Nan-Jiu 510" are with the South Sea fleet. "Dong-Jiu 332" is with the East Sea fleet.

Cable Layers

"Youzheng" class "Type 890"

No Photo available

Name	Pennant	Completed	Builder
?	?	1986	Hudong-Zhonghua Shipbuilding

Displacement. 750 tonnes
Speed. 15 knots
Dimensions. 59.4m x 9.2m x 2.8m
Complement.

Notes
Details about this vessel are very hard to come by. Her working speed is seven knots but it is not known how much cable she can lay before having to re-supply.

"Youdian" class "Type 991"

No Photo available

Name	Pennant	Completed	Builder
?	B230	1971	Guangzhou Shipbuilding
?	B233	1975	Hudong-Zhonghua Shipbuilding
?	B234	?	Hudong-Zhonghua Shipbuilding
?	B764	?	Hudong-Zhonghua Shipbuilding
?	B765	?	Hudong-Zhonghua Shipbuilding
?	B873	?	Hudong-Zhonghua Shipbuilding
?	B874	1983	Hudong-Zhonghua Shipbuilding

Displacement. 1,327 tonnes
Speed. 14 knots
Dimensions. 71.55m x 10.5m x 3.6m
Complement.

Notes
These cable layers are able to lay 400 tonnes of cable. The first vessel is a "Type 991" and the rest are "Type 991 II".

Buoy Tenders

"Yannan" class "Type 744"

No Photo available

Name	Pennant	Completed	Builder
Dongbiao	263	1980	Jiangnan Shipyard
Nanbiao	463	1980	Jiangnan Shipyard
Beibiao	982	1981	Jiangnan Shipyard
Beibiao	983	1981	Jiangnan Shipyard

Displacement. 1,750 tonnes
Speed.

Dimensions. 72.35m x 11.8m x 4m
Complement. 44

Notes
All four of these tenders are still in military service. Most other types of tenders are in civilian hands.
"Dongbiao 263", is with the East Sea fleet. "Nanbiao 463", is with the South Sea fleet. "Beibiao 982 and 983" are assigned to the North Sea fleet.

"Type 999"

No Photo available

Name	Pennant	Completed	Builder
?	?	1965	Hudong-Zhonghua Shipbuilding

Displacement. 98 tonnes
Speed. 14.5 knots

Dimensions. 28m x 5.2m x m
Complement.

Notes
This class entered service in the 1960s. Twelve of the original "Type 999" were built with several up-graded variants afterward. There is only one believed to still be in navy service.

Ocean-Going Tugs

"Tuozhong" class "Type 830"

No Photo available

Name	Pennant	Completed	Builder
Dong-Tuo	830	1977	Hudong-Zhonghua Shipbuilding
Bei-Tuo	710	1980	Hudong-Zhonghua Shipbuilding
Nan-Tuo	154	1979	Hudong-Zhonghua Shipbuilding

Displacement. 3,600 tonnes   **Dimensions.** 84.9m x 14m x 5.5m
Speed. 18.5 knots   **Complement.** 120

Notes
These large Ocean-Going Tug Boats are tasked with general tugboat duties but they are also capable of participating in the Chinese space program. They can operate as missile ranging ships and are fitted with instrumentation and satellite positioning equipment.
"Dong-Tuo", is with the East Sea fleet, "Bei-Tuo" is with the North Sea fleet and "Nan-Tuo", is with the South Sea fleet.

"Daozha" class "Type 830"

No Photo available

Name	Pennant	Completed	Builder
Dong-Tuo	890	1993	Hudong-Zhonghua Shipbuilding

Displacement. 4,000 tonnes   **Dimensions.** 84m x 12.6m x 5.4m
Speed. 18 knots   **Complement.** 125

Notes
This ship is slightly larger than the previous class. It is sometimes grouped into the "Touzhong" class because of their similarities. This ship is tasked with more duties because of the extra equipment it carries.

"Gromovoy" class "Type 802"

No Photo available

Name	Pennant	Completed	Builder
Nan-Tuo	149	1958/62	Shanghai/Dalian
Nan-Tuo	156	1958/62	Shanghai/Dalian
Nan-Tuo	166	1958/62	Shanghai/Dalian
Nan-Tuo	167	1958/62	Shanghai/Dalian
Bei-Tuo	680	1958/62	Shanghai/Dalian
Bei-Tuo	683	1958/62	Shanghai/Dalian
Bei-Tuo	684	1958/62	Shanghai/Dalian
Bei-Tuo	716	1958/62	Shanghai/Dalian
Dong-Tuo	802	1958/62	Shanghai/Dalian
Dong-Tuo	809	1958/62	Shanghai/Dalian
Dong-Tuo	811	1958/62	Shanghai/Dalian
Dong-Tuo	813	1958/62	Shanghai/Dalian
Dong-Tuo	822	1958/62	Shanghai/Dalian
Dong-Tuo	824	1958/62	Shanghai/Dalian
Dong-Tuo	827	1958/62	Shanghai/Dalian

Displacement. 795 tonnes   **Dimensions.** 45.7m x 9.5m x 4.6m
Speed. 11 knots   **Complement.** 25
Armament. 4 x 12.7mm or 14.5mm Machine guns

Notes
These tugs are based on a Soviet design. Details about exactly when each
vessel was built and by whom are hard to come by. Seventeen were originally
built with two having been decommissioned. It is very likely that more will have
gone by the time this book is published.
Those named "Nan-Tuo" are with the South Sea fleet. Those named "Bei-Tuo"
are with the North Sea fleet and those named "Dong-Tuo" are with the East Sea
fleet.

"Hujiu" class "Type 837"

[104]"Dong-Tuo 877"

Justin Zhuyan*

Name	Pennant	Completed	Builder
Dong-Tuo	836	1980s	Wuhu Shipyard
Dong-Tuo	837	1980s	Wuhu Shipyard
Dong-Tuo	842	1980s	Wuhu Shipyard
Dong-Tuo	843	1980s	Wuhu Shipyard
Dong-Tuo	875	1980s	Wuhu Shipyard
Dong-Tuo	877	1980s	Wuhu Shipyard
Bei-Tuo	622	1980s	Wuhu Shipyard
Bei-Tuo	635	1980s	Wuhu Shipyard
Bei-Tuo	711	1980s	Wuhu Shipyard
Bei-Tuo	712	1980s	Wuhu Shipyard
Bei-Tuo	717	1980s	Wuhu Shipyard
Nan-Tuo	147	1980s	Wuhu Shipyard
Nan-Tuo	155	1980s	Wuhu Shipyard
Nan-Tuo	156	1980s	Wuhu Shipyard
Nan-Tuo	164	1980s	Wuhu Shipyard
Nan-Tuo	174	1980s	Wuhu Shipyard
Nan-Tuo	175	1980s	Wuhu Shipyard
Nan-Tuo	185	1980s	Wuhu Shipyard

104
Source http://www.shipspotting.com/gallery/photo.php?lid=2349346

Displacement. 1,470 tonnes   **Dimensions.** 60.2m x 11.6m x 4.4m
Speed. 15 knots   **Complement.** 50

Notes
Twenty of these ocean-going tugs were built in the 1980s. Two were exported abroad to Bangladesh. All the vessels named "Dong-Tou" are with the East Sea fleet. The vessels named "Bei-Tuo" are with the North Sea fleet and the vessels named "Nan-Tuo" are with the South Sea fleet.

"Roslavl" class "Type 852"

[105]"Dong-Tuo 852"

Gerolf Drebes*

Name	Pennant	Completed	Builder
Nan-Tuo	161	1980s?	Chinese Shipyard
Bei-Tuo	153	1980s?	Chinese Shipyard
Bei-Tuo	159	1980s?	Chinese Shipyard
Bei-Tuo	162	1980s?	Chinese Shipyard
Bei-Tuo	163	1980s?	Chinese Shipyard
Bei-Tuo	164	1980s?	Chinese Shipyard
Bei-Tuo	168	1980s?	Chinese Shipyard
Dong-Tuo	518	1980s?	Chinese Shipyard
Dong-Tuo	604	1980s?	Chinese Shipyard
Dong-Tuo	613	1980s?	Chinese Shipyard
Dong-Tuo	618	1980s?	Chinese Shipyard
Dong-Tuo	646	1980s?	Chinese Shipyard
Dong-Tuo	707	1980s?	Chinese Shipyard
Dong-Tuo	852	1980s?	Chinese Shipyard
Dong-Tuo	853	1980s?	Chinese Shipyard
Dong-Tuo	854	1980s?	Chinese Shipyard
Dong-Tuo	862	1980s?	Chinese Shipyard
Dong-Tuo	863	1980s?	Chinese Shipyard
Dong-Tuo	867	1980s?	Chinese Shipyard

---

[105] Source http://www.shipspotting.com/gallery/photo.php?lid=1907117

Displacement. 670 tonnes   **Dimensions.** 45.7m x 9.5m x 4.6m
Speed. 12 knots   **Complement.** 28
Armament. 4 x 14.5mm guns

Notes
These tugs are the Chinese version of the Soviet designed "Roslavl" class. The
Chinese versions have a different internal arrangement. These vessels are still
in service despite their age, which cannot be verified.
Those named "Dong-Tuo" are with the East Sea fleet, those named "Bei-Tuo"
are with the North Sea fleet and the ship named "Nan-Tuo" is with the South
Sea fleet.

Naval Aviation

"J-15" Fighter

[106]"J 15"

defenceforumindia.com

Role. Fighter
Engines. 2 x WS-10A turbofans
Length. 21.9m   **Wingspan** 14.7m   **Height.** 5.9m
Max Weight. 33,000 kgs   **Range.** 2,050 miles
Max Speed. Mach 1.98   **Service Ceiling.** 65,700 feet
Crew. 1-2
Armament. 1 x 30mm cannon; 12 x hardpoints for AAM, Anti-Ship, Anti-Radiation & Bombs.

Notes
This indigenous designed fighter is based on the Russian"SU-33". One was acquired from the Ukraine in 2001 and was greatly studied. Work on the Chinese version began soon after. This aircraft is intended to be the Chinese navy's air superiority fighter for its existing and new aircraft carriers. There are estimated to be over twenty in service, having been introduced in 2013. The Chinese are confident that this aircraft is more than a match for any aircraft outside of China, with the exception of the "F-22 Raptor".

"J-8 Finback"

[107]"J-8D"

Role. Fighter
Engines. 2 x WP-13B turbojets
Length. 21.52m   **Wingspan** 9.34m   **Height.** 5.41m
Max Weight. 18,879 kgs   **Range.** 1,000 kms
Max Speed. Mach 2.2   **Service Ceiling.** 15,000m
Crew. 1
Armament. 7 x hardpoints for AAM, Anti-Ship, Anti-Radiation & Bombs.

Notes
This aircraft is designed and built in China. It is very similar, in appearance, to the Soviet made "Su-24". In fact, much of the technology used to build this aircraft, originated in the Soviet Union. This aircraft first flew in 1969 but did not enter service until 1980. By today's standards, it is obsolete and no match for modern fighters. It is still valuable as a reconnaissance aircraft because of its high speed. It is estimated that the Chinese navy still operate around 48 of the "J-8B/D/F/I" models.

---

[107]
Source https://commons.wikimedia.org/wiki/File:KampfflugzeugF-8China.jpg

"J-7 Chengdu"

[108]Pakistani "J-7"

US Air Force/Micheal B Keller

Role. Fighter
Engines. 1 x Liyang Wopen-13F turbojet
Length. 14.9m   **Wingspan** 8.32m   **Height.** 4.11m
Max Weight. 9,100 kgs   **Range.** 528 miles
Max Speed. Mach 2   **Service Ceiling.** 57,420 feet
Crew. 1
Armament. 2 x 30mm cannon; 5 x hardpoints for AAM, Anti-Ship, Anti-Radiation & Bombs.

Notes
This aircraft is the Chinese version of the very famous "MIG 21". This aircraft first flew in 1966 and over two thousand have been produced. Many have been exported to friendly states in Europe, Africa and Asia. This aircraft is entering the twilight of its service. There are reported to be about 30 in service with the Chinese naval air arm. Four of these are the two-seat trainer version. It is quite possible that all of these aircraft may have been retired by the time this book is published.

108
Source https://commons.wikimedia.org/wiki/File:Pakistani_Chengdu_J-7.JPG?uselang=en-gb

"Su-30 Flanker"

[109]"Su-30"

Dimitriy Pichigin

Role. Strike Fighter
Engines. 2 x Lyulka AL-31F turbofans
Length. 21.9m   **Wingspan** 14.7m   **Height.** 6.36m
Max Weight. 34,500 kgs   **Range.** 1,900 miles
Max Speed. Mach 2   **Service Ceiling.** 56,800 feet
Crew. 2
Armament. 1 x 30mm cannon; various hardpoints for AAM, Anti-Ship, Anti-Radiation & Bombs.

Notes
This aircraft is the Russian version of the "F 15E Strike Eagle". It is an all-weather, long-range strike aircraft and was developed after China and Russian announced a joint requirement for the aircraft. The Chinese navy operates twenty-four of these aircraft, which were delivered in 2004. It is very possible that more will be ordered to replace the "Q-5 Fantan","J-7 Chengdu" and the "J-8 Finback", as these aircraft are approaching the end of their service lives.

---

[109] Source https://commons.wikimedia.org/wiki/File:PLAAF_Sukhoi_Su-30MKK_at_Lipetsk-2.jpg?uselang=en-gb

"Xian H-6"

Aquatiger127

Role. Bomber/Maritime Strike
Engines. 2 x Xian WP8 turbojets
Length. 34.8m   **Wingspan** 33m   **Height.** 10.36m
Max Weight. 79,000 kgs   **Range.** 3,700 miles
Max Speed. 656mph   **Service Ceiling.** 42,000 feet
Crew. 4
Armament. 2 x 23mm cannons; 6 x hardpoints for Anti-Ship missiles & Bombs.

Notes
This is the Chinese version of the Soviet "Tupolev Tu-16". It was built by the
Xian aircraft company and first flew in 1959. It is thought that it did not enter
service until 1968. Production followed at a slow rate and by the 1990s, it was
estimated that only 150 had been built. 30 of those aircraft, (H-6D), are believed
to still be in Chinese naval service.
This aircraft was China's long-range, strategic nuclear bomber but over the
years, it has had to adapt to other roles because of modern air-defence
measures. One role is of airborne tanker. Reports say there are three in this
role.

---

[110] Source https://commons.wikimedia.org/wiki/File:PLAAF_Xian_H-6M_Over_Changzhou.jpg

"Q-5 Fantan"

[111]"Q-5"

Patc045

Role. Ground Attack
Engines. 2 x Liming Wopen-6A turbojets
Length. 15.65m   **Wingspan** 9.68m   **Height.** 4.33m
Max Weight. 11,830 kgs   **Range.** 1,200 miles
Max Speed. 752mph   **Service Ceiling.** 54,133 feet
Crew. 1
Armament. 2 x 23mm cannons; 10 x hardpoints for 2,000kg of ordnance

Notes
This Chinese-built aircraft is based on the Soviet "MIG 19". It first flew in 1965
and entered service in 1970. Over one thousand were produced, with most of
them being operated by China. Some were exported to Bangladesh, Pakistan
and Myanmar. There were plans to upgrade these aircraft with Western
avionics but this was cancelled after the Tiananmen Square incident of 1985.
These aircraft are being withdrawn from service but there are estimated to still
be 30 in service with the Chinese navy. They may have been retired by the time
this book is published.

"SH-5 Harbin"

¹¹²"SH-5"   tienvijftien

Role. Maritime Patrol
Engines. 4 x Dongan WJ 5A turboprops
Length. 38.9m   **Wingspan** 36m   **Height.** 9.79m
Max Weight. 45,000 kgs   **Range.** 2,955 miles
Max Speed. 345mph   **Service Ceiling.** 33,629 feet
Crew. 8
Armament.4 x hardpoints for 6,000kg of ordnance

Notes
This is one of the very few types of Seaplanes in service anywhere in the world.
The prototype first flew in 1976 but production did not start until 1984. A total of
seven were built, with production ending in 1986. The Chinese navy received
four aircraft but one has since been rebuilt as a fire-fighting aircraft.

"Shaanxi Y-8"

Alert5

Role. Transport/Reconnaissance/Maritime Patrol
Engines. 4 x Zhuzhou Wojiang-6 turboprops
Length. 34.02m   **Wingspan** 38m   **Height.** 11.16m
Max Weight. 61,000 kgs   **Range.** 3,485 miles
Max Speed. 410mph   **Service Ceiling.** 34,000 feet
Crew. 2-5

Notes
This is a medium-sized transport aircraft, which was designed and built in China and is based on the Soviet, "Antonov An-12". The prototype first flew in 1974, with production beginning in 1981. Approximately 170 had been built by 2010, with many of them receiving upgrades and modernisations, to keep them operational.
Several aircraft have been converted to act as Maritime patrol and Reconnaissance aircraft. Sources suggest that there are four transport, six reconnaissance and four maritime patrol aircraft in Chinese navy service.

"Y-5 Colt"

[114]Civilian "Y-5"

Xu Zheng

Role. Transport
Engines. 1 x Shvetsov Ash-62IR radial engine
Length. 12.4m   **Wingspan** 18.2m   **Height.** 4.1m
Max Weight. 5,440 kgs   **Range.** 525 miles
Max Speed. 160mph   **Service Ceiling.** 14,750 feet
Crew. 1-2

Notes
This is one of the oldest aircraft, which is still in production, anywhere in the
world. It first flew in 1947 as the "Antonov An-2" and production continued until
1991, when over thirteen thousand had been built. China also began producing
this aircraft, on licence as the "Y-5" and production is continuing. Twelve
passengers or a payload of over two tonnes can be carried. It is thought that
there are about fifty of these planes still in service with the Chinese navy.

---

[114] Source https://commons.wikimedia.org/wiki/File:Changjiang_General_Aviation_Shijiazhuang_Y-
5B(D)_at_Fuzhou_Changle_Airport.jpg

"Y-7"

[115]Civilian "Y-7"

Kok Chwee Sim

Role. Transport
Engines. 2 x Dongan WJ5A turboprop
Length. 24.2m   **Wingspan** 29.6m   **Height.** 8.5m
Max Weight. 21,800 kgs   **Range.** 1,231 miles
Max Speed. 313mph   **Service Ceiling.** 28,700 feet
Crew. 3

Notes
This aircraft is the Chinese version of the Soviet "Antonov An-24". China
purchased the "An-24" and then sought a production licence to build them in
China. This licence was granted in 1966 and the first Chinese "Y-7" flew in
1970. Production began in 1977 and has proceeded at a slow pace with just
over 100 of these aircraft having been built to date. There are four "Y-7s" and
six "Y-7H's" in service with the Chinese navy.

Source https://commons.wikimedia.org/wiki/File:President_Airlines_XAC_Y7-100C_KCS.jpg?uselang=en-gb

"Yak-42"

[116]Civilian "Yak-42"

Ole Simon

Role. Transport
Engines. 3 x Lotarev D-36 turbofans
Length. 36.38m   **Wingspan** 34.88m   **Height.** 9.83m
Max Weight. 57,500 kgs   **Range.** 2,458 miles
Max Speed. 503mph   **Service Ceiling.** 31,500 feet
Crew. 3

Notes
This airliner was produced in the Soviet Union and Russia between 1979 and
2003. Almost two hundred have been built and exported. It is thought that the
Chinese navy operates two of these planes for basic transport duties.

---

[116]
Source https://commons.wikimedia.org/wiki/File:Lviv_Airlines_Yakovlev_Yak-42_Simon.jpg?uselang=en-gb

"JJ-6" Trainer

[117]"J-6"   Alert5

Role. Trainer
Engines. 2 x Liming Wopen-6A turbojets
Length. 12.54m   **Wingspan** 9.2m   **Height.** 3.9m
Max Weight. 7,560 kgs   **Range.** 400 miles
Max Speed. 960mph   **Service Ceiling.** 58,700 feet
Crew. 2

Notes
This aircraft is the Chinese version of the Soviet "MIG 19". The "MIG 19" was not in Soviet service for long but the "J-6" stayed in Chinese production from 1958 to 1981. All of the fighter versions have been retired but the two-seater trainer version is still in service. There are reported to be fourteen still active in navy service.

---

[117] Source https://commons.wikimedia.org/wiki/File:Shenyang_J-6.jpg

"CJ-6"

¹¹⁸"CJ-6"

Valder 137

Role. Trainer
Engines. 1 x Zhuzhou HS6A radial engine
Length. 8.46m   **Wingspan** 10.22m   **Height.** 3.3m
Max Weight. 1,400 kgs   **Range.** 425 miles
Max Speed. 185mph   **Service Ceiling.** 20,000+ feet
Crew. 2

Notes
Almost forty of these trainers are in service with the Chinese navy. This plane was developed from the Soviet "Yak-18". When China needed a trainer, they found the "Yak-18" did not have the performance required; therefore, they built a new aircraft along its lines. It was introduced in 1960 and over two thousand have been built.

118 Source https://commons.wikimedia.org/wiki/File:Nanchang_CJ-6A_N285CJ_Takeoff_01_TICO_13March2010_(14412718440).jpg?uselang=en-gb

Helicopters

"Z-18"

"Z-18"

Allen Zhao

Role. ASW/Transport
Engines. 3 x WZ-6C turboshafts
Length. 23m   **Rotor Diameter** 19m   **Height.** 7m
Max Weight. 13.8 tonnes   **Range.** 900 kms
Max Speed. 336 kmph   **Service Ceiling.** 9,000m
Crew. 2

Notes
This large helicopter is the naval version of the "Z-8". It has been developed by the Changhe Aircraft Company and entered service in 2014. It is being produced in large numbers to replace the "Z-8" and to equip the navy with the necessary helicopters during its massive expansion.

This machine has more powerful engines than the "Z-8" and can carry a heavier payload of 4,000kgs, internally and 5,000kgs externally. 27 passengers can be accommodated or 14 stretchers. These machines are currently being deployed on the "Liaoning" aircraft carrier and will certainly be deployed on the new amphibious ships that the Chinese navy is constructing.

"Z-8 Super Frelon"

120"Z-8"

Rob Schleiffert

Role. ASW/Transport
Engines. 3 x Turbomeca Turmo IIIC turboshafts
Length. 23.03m   **Rotor Diameter** 18.90m   **Height.** 6.66m
Max Weight. 13,000 kgs   **Range.** 632 miles
Max Speed. 155 mph   **Service Ceiling.** 10,325
Crew. 5
Armament. Torpedoes or Anti-ship missiles.

Notes
The first flight of this helicopter was in 1962 and it was produced by the French company, Aerospatiale. In 1977/1978, China purchased 13 of these machines, some were the Anti-submarine variant and some the Search & Rescue type. They were the first helicopter to operate from the deck of a Chinese warship. It is not known how many of these machines are still in operation, as they are being replaced by the new "Z-18".

"Kamov KA-28"

[121]"Kamov 28"   defenceforumindia.com

Role. Anti-submarine
Engines. 2 x Isotov TV3-117 turboshaft
Length. 11.3m   **Rotor Diameter.** 15.8m   **Height.** 5.5m
Max Weight. 12,000 kgs   **Range.** 609 miles
Max Speed. 168 mph   **Service Ceiling.** 16,404 feet
Crew. Max 6
Armament. Various torpedoes and mines

Notes
This is the anti-submarine version of the very successful "Kamov" helicopter. It is the improved version of the "KA-25". Over 250 have been built for Russia, China, Vietnam, South Korea and India. The Chinese acquired five machines to operate from their "Sovremenny" class destroyers. Nine more were purchased in 2009 as the Chinese fleet began to expand.

"Kamov KA-31"

"Ka-31"

Aleksander Markin

Role. Early warning
Engines. 2 x Isotov TV3-117VMAR turboshaft
Length. 12.5m   **Rotor Diameter.** 14.5m   **Height.** 5.6m
Max Weight. 12,200 kgs   **Range.** 600 kms
Max Speed. 166 mph   **Service Ceiling.** 11,483 feet
Crew. 2

Notes
This helicopter is the early warning version of the very successful "Kamov" type
helicopter. It is of Soviet origin, going back to the Cold War. It was designed as
a result of the cancellation of the "Antonov AN-71" AWACS. As an early warning
aircraft was still needed, "Kamov" built an early-warning helicopter. It first flew in
1983 and entered service in 1995. The radar is slung beneath the fuselage and
is lowered into position when operated. The Chinese navy has ordered this
machine to operate from its existing aircraft carrier. Just how many will be
purchased remains to be seen.

122
Source https://commons.wikimedia.org/wiki/File:Ka-31_(4288619876).jpg?uselang=en-gb

"Harbin Z-9"

[123]"Z-9"

Owen King

Role. Utility
Engines. 2 x Zhuzhou Aeroengine Factory WZ-8A turboshaft
Length. 12.11m   **Rotor Diameter.** 11.94m   **Height.** 4.01m
Max Weight. 4,100 kgs   **Range.** 621 miles
Max Speed. 190 mph   **Service Ceiling.** 14,764 feet
Crew. 1-2

Notes
This helicopter is the Chinese version of the French "Dauphin". The first version flew in 1981, after a deal with Aerospatiale. Most of that particular helicopter was made with French-supplied components. By 1992, the "Z-9B" was flown and that was 70% Chinese. This machine entered Chinese service in 1994 and over two hundred have so far, been built.

"S-100" Drone

defenceforumindia.com

In 2010, the Chinese navy purchased 18 of these drones from the Austrian company, Schiebel. These machines can travel at a top speed of 222mph and have a range of 180kms. They can be carried and launched by any ship, as the full length of this machine is only 3.4m.

124
Source http://defenceforumindia.com/forum/threads/china-military-photos-videos.3157/page-105

Naval Weapons

Ballistic Missiles

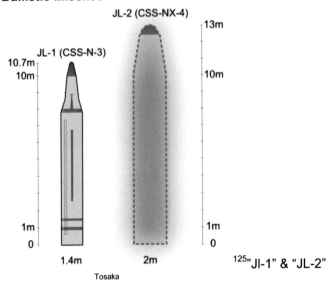

Tosaka

^{125}JI-1" & "JL-2"

Research and development for the "JL-1", began in 1967 and steadily progressed until the first sea-launch in 1982. It was first deployed on a "Type 092" SSBN in 1986. The missile is 10.7m in length and 1.4m diameter. It can carry one nuclear warhead to a range of 2,500kms.

The "JL-2" is the next generation of missile. It began development in the 1980s and the first sea-launch was in 2001. It is 13m long and has a diameter of 2m. It carries 3 to 4 nuclear warheads and has a range of 8,000kms. It is deployed on the "Type 094" SSBN and has the range to attack India and the USA.

Torpedoes

Brokensphere

[126]"Type 53"

This torpedo is of Russian origin and used to equip the "Kilo" class submarine. It probably equips most of China's other submarine force. The torpedo is 7.2m long and has a diameter of 533mm. It carries a 678lb warhead out to a range of about 20,000 yards, at a speed of 45 knots.

One Half 3544

[127]"Shkval"

This Russian torpedo is thought to be in service with the Chinese navy. This is the world's fastest torpedo, with a speed of 200knots. Unfortunately, it only has a range of about 10kms, making the submarine carrying it, very vulnerable. Its main advantage is that once fired, its target has no escape.

---

[126] Source https://commons.wikimedia.org/wiki/File:53-65K_torpedo_MW.JPG

[127] Source https://commons.wikimedia.org/wiki/File:Shkval.jpg

[128]"YU-1"

Max Smith

This torpedo is the first steam-powered torpedo built by China. It is a development of the "Type 53" and is 7.8m long and has diameter of 533mm. It carries a 400kg warhead to a range of 9km, at a speed between 39 and 50 knots. Even though it first entered service in 1971, it is still operational and continually updated.

[129]"YU-2"

Max Smith

This torpedo was developed before the "YU-1" and is still in Chinese service. It is 4m long and 450mm in diameter. It carries a 200kg warhead to a range of 1km at 70 knots. There is no chance of the delivery submarine or aircraft's survival because it would have get so near to its target. These torpedoes have been converted to act as mines in the waters around China.

"YU-3"
This torpedo entered service with the Chinese navy in 1984. It is 7.8m long and 533mm in diameter. It carries a 205kg warhead to a range of 13km, at a speed of 35 knots and is carried by most of China's submarine force.

"YU-4"
This torpedo was developed alongside the "YU-1". It took longer to bring into service, with service entry in 1982. The range was only 6km, so an improved model was built and entered service in 1987, with a 15km range. Each torpedo is 7.75m long and 533mm in diameter. It carries a 309kg warhead.

---

[128] Source https://commons.wikimedia.org/wiki/File:Yu-1_Torpedo_-_3_merged_photographs.jpg
[129] Source https://commons.wikimedia.org/wiki/File:Yu-2_Torpedo.jpg

"YU-5"
This torpedo is the first Chinese developed, wire-guided torpedo. It is also the first Chinese developed anti-submarine torpedoes to be deployed on conventional submarines. Development began in the early 1970s, with service introduction in 1989. It is 7.8m long and 533mm in diameter. It has a 400kg warhead and a range of 30kms.

"YU-6"
This is the Chinese version of the American "Mk 48", heavyweight torpedo. It began development in 1995 and entered service in 2005. It has a range of 45km and a speed of 65 knots. It can be fired using acoustic guidance or wire-guided. It has most likely replaced some of the older torpedoes in service, already mentioned.

"YU-7"
This is a lightweight torpedo, which is the Chinese equivalent of the US "Mk 46". Several "Mk 46" torpedoes were recovered by Chinese fishermen and used as the basis for China to develop its own. Development began in 1984 and service introduction was in 1994. The torpedo is ship-launched and 2.6m in length. It is 324mm in diameter, has a speed of 43 knots carrying a 45kg warhead, and has a range of 14kms.

"YU-8"
This is an electrically-powered torpedo, which is sometimes called a counterpart to the fuelled "YU-6". Not many details are available about this weapon. It is capable of being launched from surface or sub-surface platforms.

"YU-11"
This is the follow-on torpedo to the "YU-7". Development began in 2002, with service entry in 2015. It has more range and is faster than the "YU-7".

"ET 34" & "ET 36"
These two torpedoes are variants of the "YU-5". They are 6.6m long and 533mm in diameter. The "ET 34" has slightly more range, at 25km and is slightly faster, at 42 knots.

"650mm Type 65"

This torpedo is reported to be in service with the Chinese navy. It is hard to get a definite answer because of Chinese secrecy. It would not be surprising considering China's naval build-up and its attitude towards the American navy. The "Type 65" torpedo would be the biggest in the Chinese Navy's vast arsenal. It is from the days of the Soviet Navy and was produced to sink the US Navy's aircraft carriers. It is supposed to have the ability to sink an aircraft carrier with one torpedo, instead of many. Special torpedo tubes have to be fitted to the carrying submarine but these also come with a lining to allow more conventional "533mm" torpedoes to be fired from these tubes. Most of the Russian Navy's submarine force has the capability to carry this torpedo and now, according to reports, does the Chinese navy.

The torpedo has a length of 9.14m and a range of 100km's, at a speed of approximately 25 knots. It can travel 50km's, at a speed of 50 knots and carries a warhead of 557kg of high explosive or a nuclear weapon.

Guns

defenceforumindia.com

[130]"Type 730", "30mm"

This is the Chinese version of the "Dutch made "Goalkeeper" system. It can fire 4,200 rounds-per-minute to a range of 3kms. It is deployed on frigates and other surface vessels of the Chinese navy.

defenceforumindia.com

[131]"30mm" Gatling

This type of Gatling gun can be seen on most Soviet -era built warships from aircraft carriers to patrol boats. China is also a major operator of this weapon. It is designed to tackle small surface craft, low flying aircraft and sea-skimming missiles. It can fire 6,000 rounds-per-minute, with an effective range of over a mile.

[132]"AK-630"

Badgerass

This is a "Close-In-Weapon" system, which is the Russian Navy's equivalent of the US Navy's "Phalanx". It is a "30mm", 6-barrelled gun with a firing rate of at least 4,000 rounds-per-minute. It has an effective range of 4,000m's and is deployed on the largest surface unit down to the smallest. China has acquired this weapon to equip its surface vessels.

[133]"Kashtan 30mm"

Emmanuel L

This is a "Close-In-Weapon" system of Russian origin. It is sometimes deployed as a combined gun and missile system. The gun version has two 6-barrelled guns, which are radar controlled. It can fire 9,000 rounds-per-minute, out to an effective range of 4,000m's. It is found on the largest surface units and the new frigate-size vessels, which the Chinese Navy is now building.

---

[132] Source https://commons.wikimedia.org/wiki/File:Duetak630m2.jpg
[133] Source http://www.shipspotting.com/gallery/photo.php?lid=2103758

¹³⁴"76mm AK-176"

US Navy/Don S Montgomery

This gun is from the Soviet era. It is the Russian equivalent of the "Otobreda 76mm". It is very effective against surface targets, low flying aircraft and sea-skimming missiles. It can fire 120 rounds-per-minute, out to a maximum range of 15km's. It is an automatic system, which is belt fed. A normal belt is 152 rounds.

¹³⁵"Twin 37mm"

defenceforumindia.com

This weapon was developed from a Soviet weapon of the same calibre. It is a fully automatic system, deployed on many Chinese surface vessels. It can fire 375 rounds-per-minute against surface and airborne targets.

134
Source https://commons.wikimedia.org/wiki/File:Hiddensee_AK-176_gun.jpg?uselang=en-gb
135
Source http://defenceforumindia.com/forum/threads/china-military-photos-videos.3157/page-134

[136]30mm gun

This weapon can be remotely or manually operated. It is effective against surface, airborne or sea-skimming targets and is deployed on many of China's newer warships.

[137]"Twin 100mm"

This gun was first developed in the 1970s. It was designed to replace the old Soviet weapons which had been in service for many years. Details about rates of fire and range are hard to come by.

---

[136] Source http://defenceforumindia.com/forum/threads/china-military-photos-videos.3157/page-93

[137] Source http://defenceforumindia.com/forum/threads/china-military-photos-videos.3157/page-25

[138]"AK-230"

Esquilo

This "30mm" weapon is based on the "30mm Gatling". It is basically the same mount but with twin "30mm" guns instead of a 6 barrelled Gatling. Each barrel can fire 1,000 rounds-per-minute, out to an effective range of 4km's. It is designed to engage small surface craft, low flying aircraft and sea-skimming missiles. It is deployed on surface vessels of every size and type.

[139]"14.5mm"

tretyak_2004@mail.ru

This is a heavy calibre weapon, which is still deployed on some of the older units of the Chinese Navy. It is used against surface and air-borne targets and can fire 600 rounds-per-minute, out to an effective range of 3,000m.

[138] Source https://commons.wikimedia.org/wiki/File:Forward_AK-230,_Keih%C3%A4ssalmi.jpg

[139] Source
https://upload.wikimedia.org/wikipedia/commons/1/1a/%D0%9A%D0%BE%D1%80%D0%B0%D0%B1%D0%B5%D0%BB%D1%8C%D0%BD%D0%B0%D1%8F_%D0%BF%D1%83%D0%BB%D0%B5%D0%BC%D0%B5%D1%82%D0%BD%D0%B0%D1%8F_%D1%83%D1%81%D1%82%D0%B0%D0%BD%D0%BE%D0%B2%D0%BA%D0%B0_2%D0%9C-5.JPG

[140]"AK-130 130mm"

Mr Jack

This is a dual-purpose weapon, designed to engage surface and airborne targets. It can fire 35 rounds-per-minute, to an effective range of 22kms. It can be operated either automatically or manually and is deployed on "Sovremenny" class destroyers.

[141]"100mm"

Boleslav1

This weapon is the Chinese version of a French artillery piece. It was developed to make it fit with Chinese warships and to make it compatible with Chinese technology. It is capable of firing 90 rounds-per-minute of different types of ammunition.

---

[140] Source https://commons.wikimedia.org/wiki/File:AK-130_on_destroyer_%C2%ABNastoychivyy%C2%BB_in_Baltiysk,_2008_(1).jpg?uselang=en-gb

[141] Source https://commons.wikimedia.org/wiki/File:Type_052B_Guangzhou_in_Leningrad.jpg

Anti-Ship Missiles

[142]"C-801"

defenceforumindia.com

This missile is the first of the "C-800" generation. It was developed in the 1980s and is the missile several others are based on. It is 5.8m long and 36cm in diameter. It carries a 165kg warhead to a range of 40kms. It has a solid rocket engine, which propels it to Mach 0.75.

[143]"C-802"

defenceforumindia.com

This is an updated version of the "C-801". The "C-802" has had its range extended to 120kms. It carries a 165kg warhead at a speed of Mach 0.9. The missile is 6.3m in length and a diameter of 36cm. It travels just above the surface and carries its own anti-jamming electronics. According to sources, it has a 98% chance of hitting its target.

[142] Source http://defenceforumindia.com/forum/threads/china-military-photos-videos.3157/page-135
[143] Source http://defenceforumindia.com/forum/threads/china-military-photos-videos.3157/page-116

[144]"C-803"

This missile began to be developed in 1994 and is the next in the "C-800" family. Reportedly, development began as a counter to a Taiwanese missile. This missile carries a 190kg warhead and has a range of 180kms. It has a length of 6.85m and a diameter of 36cm.

[145]"C-601"

This is the Chinese version of the Soviet "Silkworm" missile. It is very basic and very bulky. It is 6.5m long and has diameter of 0.76m. It carries a 513kg warhead to a range of 150kms. It is propelled by a rocket booster and liquid fuelled engine at a speed of Mach 0.8.

---

[144] Source http://defenceforumindia.com/forum/threads/china-military-photos-videos.3157/page-116

[145] Source http://defenceforumindia.com/forum/threads/china-military-photos-videos.3157/page-16

This is a sea-skimming cruise missile and is believed to have entered service in 2005, deployed on many of China's surface warships. It has a range in excess of 280km at a speed of Mach 0.8. The warhead size can range between 210kg to 480 kg of high explosive.

[147]"Kh-35"

Allocer

The "Kh-35" or "SS-N-25" is one of the many new missiles from Russia, which are beginning to equip the very latest Chinese warships. It is anti-ship missile, which has a range of 300kms and a speed of Mach 0.8. It is kerosene propelled and has a "shaped charge" warhead of 310lbs of high explosive.

[146] Source http://defenceforumindia.com/forum/threads/china-military-photos-videos.3157/page-116
[147] Source https://commons.wikimedia.org/wiki/File:Kh-35E_fol_maks2009.jpg

[148]"3M-54 Klub"
Allocer

The "3M-54" or "SS-N-27" is another new anti-ship missile from Russia. This missile can be launched from a surface ship using a vertical launch system or by a submerged submarine, via a torpedo tube. It can also be launched from an aircraft. The length, speed and range all depend from which platform the missile is launched. Length goes from 6.2m to 8.22m. Speed ranges from Mach 0.8 to Mach 2.9. Range varies from 200kms to 660kms. A cruise missile variant has a range of 2,500kms.

"C 701"
This is the first of the "C-700" family of missiles. It entered service in 1989 and has spawned several successors. It can be launched from a surface warship or an aircraft and is 2.5m long and 18cm in diameter. It has a 29kg warhead and a range of 25km. It is a sea-skimming missile and travels at a speed of Mach 0.8.

[149]"C-704"
IDF

This missile has been developed to attack ships with a displacement of 4,000 tonnes maximum. It carries a 130 kg warhead and has a range of 35 kms.

---

[148] Source https://commons.wikimedia.org/wiki/File:3M-54E1.jpg
[149] Source https://commons.wikimedia.org/wiki/File:Flickr_-_Israel_Defense_Forces_-_Weaponry_Found_On-Board_the_%22Victoria%22_(1).jpg

"C-705"
This missile looks like a smaller "C 602". It still looks like a cruise missile and has a range of 170kms. It has a 110 to 130kg warhead and is designed to attack ships with a maximum displacement of 3,000 tonnes.

"FL-7"
This missile has been in production since the 1980s. It is a supersonic anti-ship missile, which can be launched by a surface warship or an aircraft. It has a range of only 32km and a speed of Mach 1.4. This missile is in the process of being withdrawn as newer, more advanced missiles are produced.

"FL-8", "FL-9" & "FL-10"
These missiles are the land-based versions of the "FL-7". Each missile is designed to be launched from coastal batteries and engage enemy vessels. Each missile is an updated version of the preceding one.

"C-301"
This is a very large coastal defence missile. It is land based and is used to engage enemy ships to a range of 180kms. It is 9.85m in length and has a wingspan of 2.24m. It is basically a small ballistic missile, travels at Mach 2.5 and carries a 500kg warhead. It is powered by four booster jets in the early phase and, when it reaches Mach 1.8, the Ram jet starts up and powers the missile.

"C-302"
This the first improved version of the "C-301" missile. It never entered mass production, as it was not deemed worthwhile. Several missiles were in service but it is unclear if they have remained or been replaced.

"C-303"
This last version of the "C-301" is more of a ballistic missile than the previous two. Instead of flying at a very low altitude, it climbs to 20km high and when the target is in sight, it dives onto it. This makes the impact much more devastating. This missile has also entered production but on a limited scale.

Surface-to-Air Missiles

[150]"SA-N-12"

This is a surface-to-air missile, which is of Russian origin. It is launched on the Chinese version of the US "Mk 13" launcher. The missile has a range of 38km and can engage low and high altitude targets.

[151]"FL 3000"

櫻井千一

This missile system is similar to the US designed "Rolling Airframe Missile" system. It can fire eight missiles from its launcher before it needs to be reloaded. Each missile is 2m long and has a maximum range of 9kms. It is currently deployed on corvette-sized vessels.

---

[150] Source http://defenceforumindia.com/forum/threads/china-military-photos-videos.3157/page-135

[151] Source https://commons.wikimedia.org/wiki/File:Type_056_corvette_FL-3000N_8-round_SAM_launcher.jpg

[152]"HHQ-9"

defenceforumindia.com

This is the naval version of the "HQ-9" missile. This missile is deployed in "Vertical Launch" tubes, aboard several types of Chinese warships. They are in circular magazines, each carrying six missiles. The number of magazines depends on the size of the carrying vessel. The missile is 6.8m long and travels at a speed of Mach 4.2. It is two-stage missile, which can engage low and high altitude targets.

[153]"HQ-16"

defenceforumindia.com

This is the naval version the Russian "Buk" missile. The missile is usually deployed in eight cell launchers. How many cells are on-board each ship, depends on the ship's size. This missile is capable of engaging low and high altitude targets.

152
   Source http://defenceforumindia.com/forum/threads/china-military-photos-videos.3157/page-132
153
   Source http://defenceforumindia.com/forum/threads/china-military-photos-videos.3157/page-115

[154]"HQ-7"

This is a very basic, compared to some systems, point-defence missile system. Each launcher has eight, ready-to-fire missiles. Each missile is 3m in length and 0.154m in diameter. It has a range of 15,000m at a speed of Mach 2.3.

---

[154] Source http://defenceforumindia.com/forum/threads/china-military-photos-videos.3157/page-25